# Geocaching GPS:

## Great Personal Stories of Geocaching Firsts

Edited by Kimberly Eldredge

*For Ben.*

# *Contents*

# Acknowledgements

Special thanks to our sponsor, Oakcoins for helping to make this book possible. You can find them at Oakcoins.com

Big thanks as well to the world-wide geocaching community, especially the staff and volunteers at Geocaching.com for all their work to sure this game runs smoothly and is fun for all.

I'd also like to thank the 50 wonderful geocachers in the book – without you and your families this book never would have happened. I appreciate all you do to place caches, support each other, and the time and effort you put into your story. I'm so proud of you all and honored to be your editor and a geocacher in your company.

And, as always, thanks for their support and tireless "cheerleader" effort goes to my folks, Bruce and Rose Eldredge, and my soul-mate, Ben. Here's to many happy years for geocaching for us all!

# The Story Behind 'Geocaching GPS'

I've been geocaching for a long time – like since 2008 and I've run a geocaching blog at FindYourGeocache.com since 2009. Something that has always struck me is the wonderful stories geocachers have. Sure, there's the "There's great swag in this cache" or the "Muggles were EVERYWHERE around that cache" type stories, but there were even more stories of how a game of "Using multi-million dollar satellites to find Tupperware® in the woods" has changed lives.

My life's purpose is to help people write and publish their books – so what better use of my gifts and talent than to do the same for the geocaching community?

The first year of Geocaching GPS was amazing – Volume 1 had stories from around the globe and created my own personal global community of geocachers. Friends that I felt I really got to know through their stories – and it was my honor to edit them and publish them for the world.

So in early 2016, it made sense to start to put together Volume 2. Again this year, the stories in this book were collected via a free writing contest. I was looking to expand our reach with more authors (which happened) and to bring you stories that were even richer and with more excitement. The wonderful response to this project from the geocaching community (again!) completely blew my mind! I know many geocachers and muggles alike who are thrilled to be finally holding this book in their hands.

For the majority of the authors in this book, this is their first publication. The thing they all have in common, however, is that they all have an amazing, feel-good geocaching story to share.

Most of the authors included in this anthology are not professional authors. Their stories have been lightly edited for clarity, but the words are their own. For a few of the authors, English is NOT their first language so the story was edited for clarity but also to leave the voice intact. The unusual turn of phrase or awkwardness is intentional to make sure their personality comes through!

I'm honored to have been entrusted with their words, their stories, and their messages. I hope you enjoy reading "Geocaching GPS" as much as we all enjoyed creating it for you.

*Kim Eldredge*

Kim Eldredge, TippySheep


*Editor's Note:* Under the story's title, you'll find both the real name of the author and their geocaching name.

As you read this book, there may be terms you don't recognize, like Muggle or GZ, that are unique to the game of geocaching. Please find an explanation of these terms at the end of the book. Additional information about geocaching can be found in the "Extras" section.

If you'd like to find a list of all the geocaches mentioned in this book, you can find it at www.GeocachingGPS.com under the section for Volume 2.

# What is Geocaching?

*Just in case you've never heard of this game or received this book as a gift!*

Geocaching is a high-tech treasure hunting game played throughout the world by adventure seekers equipped with GPS devices. The basic idea is to locate hidden containers, called "geocaches" or just simply "caches", and then share your experiences online.

Other geocachers obtain the coordinates and seek out the cache using their handheld GPS devices. The finding geocachers record their find in the logbook and then they also record the find online.

Geocaching is enjoyed by people from all age groups, with a strong sense of community and support for the environment.

## Geocache Containers

A geocaching container should be water-proof, critter-proof, and well hidden. It can be anything from a micro-cache to a container large enough for "swag". Geocache container sizes range from film canisters often called "microcaches," too small to hold anything more than a tiny paper log, to five-gallon buckets or even larger containers.

Geocache containers are often camouflaged with paint or tape to make them blend in with their surroundings. Imagine finding a film canister, spray-painted green and brown, in a forest! With a GPS to help, that is exactly what geocachers do every day.

For the traditional geocache, a geocacher will hide a waterproof container, containing a log book (with pen or pencil) and trinkets or some sort of treasures, then note the cache's coordinates. These coordinates, along with other details of the location, are posted on the Geocaching.com website.

## Geocache Prizes or "Swag"

"Swag" is the goodies left inside a geocache. The rule is: take something of equal value to what you are leaving. You don't have to take anything if you're more into the thrill of the find.

Typical cache treasures are not high in monetary value but may hold personal value to the finder. Aside from the logbook, common cache contents are unusual coins or currency, small toys, ornamental buttons, geocoins, or other small items

Occasionally, higher value items are included in geocaches, normally reserved for the first to find, or "FTF", or in locations which are harder to reach.

Speaking of "FTF", geocachers use a type of "shorthand" to make notes to other geocachers in the logbook. Examples are: TNLN (Took Nothing, Left Nothing); SL (Signed Log); and TFTF (Thanks For The Find.)

# Trackable Items

Attach a Travel Bug tag to an item, create a mission for its travels, and then place the item into a geocache. As your Travel Bug moves from geocache to geocache, picking up stories and photos along the way, you can live vicariously through the bug's adventures!

Cachers who initially place a Travel Bug or Geocoin often assign specific goals for their trackable items. One such goal could be to pass it westward across the continent.

Geocoins work similarly to Travel Bugs in that they are trackable and can travel the world. Some geocoins are often created as signature items by geocachers and can also be used as collectibles. Collectable geocoins are not trackable.

6

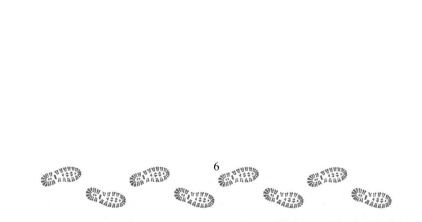

# *Journey to the Center of Black Point*

Kelly Rysten
*El Pollo Loco Gang*

The big 5/5. Some people never find one. I debated with myself about the wisdom of looking for a geocache rated 5/5. Given my propensity for sun stroke and the fact that I had my eye on a four wheel drive road, followed by a hike to a slot canyon, maybe this wasn't the cache for me. However, TSPI and I had a 1,000th milestone coming up. We had to do something special for our 1,000th milestone, and this cache met all my qualifications for a fun time. It was out of town. It was up a four wheel drive road. There were rocks to climb on, a canyon to find. And, after much research, it didn't look too difficult. How could anybody not find a canyon?

A Claustrophobic's Nightmare/Just Say NO to Crack (GCK2AW) had just enough quirkiness and adventure in the title to really tempt me. I love caves. I would attempt to squeeze into any claustrophobia inducing spot I could fit into, if there was a guarantee I would get back out.

It was June and our wedding anniversary lining up with our 1,000th find gave me extra incentive to plan a trip so I began a campaign to take a long weekend trip to Mammoth Lakes and

Bodie Ghost Town with a drive through Yosemite, oh yes, and a small detour to find the milestone cache.

June is not the best time of the year for someone who has trouble in hot weather to visit the eastern Sierras. I nearly passed out looking for Fossil Falls. My GPS said I was 3 feet from the cache when I announced I was walking to the truck, no questions asked. I had to go find shade and water before I couldn't find shade or water.

We were a little smarter when we went to the crack. We got an early start. We ate breakfast. We brought plenty of water. I wore my hat. I hate hats but I thought this occasion was important enough to risk hat hair. I think I even brought a damp towel in case of meltdown.

A Claustrophobic's Nightmare is inside a hill. The hill overlooks Mono Lake, a desert lake with beautiful and unusual tufa rock formations. We drove from Mammoth Lakes and located the dirt road leading in. We only found one spot along the road that required four wheel drive. It was a sandy hill that looks like a ski run full of moguls. The moguls are different each time a car goes over them because each pass rearranges the sand. We did not have four wheel drive. We had a two wheel drive Ford Explorer. TSPI had plenty of experience with rough desert roads to make up for the lack of four wheel drive. We needed two attempts to climb the hill. One taught us that the sand was unstable and the moguls were temporary. After rearranging the moguls I hopped out to take pictures of attempt number two. Dirt and rocks flew all around the SUV as it lurched over and into the moguls. The tires spun, sometimes uselessly, but eventually TSPI made it to the top of the hill where we held a small celebration. Obstacle number one, check!

Obstacle number two was to find the slot canyon. We parked about a half mile from the hill at the end of the road. Luckily temperatures were only in the 80's and there was a breeze off the lake. Conditions were in my favor. Unfortunately, we couldn't see the slot canyon from the end of the road, so we relied on our GPRs to guide us there. Our GPSs led us about a quarter mile out of our way before we decided the entrance to the canyon had to be northwest of us. We followed the base of Black Point until we came to a small opening. I didn't even think it was the slot canyon. I just thought it was a rock, and rocks are meant to be climbed, so I climbed it. Whoa, behind the rock was an opening. And it kept going. At this point it didn't matter if the opening was our goal or not, I had to follow this opening to see where it went. It looked like a dusty trail through solid rock walls. I didn't feel claustrophobic, but I bet some people do.

For most of the walk through the slot canyon we could touch both walls of the canyon at the same time. The walls of the fissure were rugged and pocked by interesting hidey holes. Birds scolded us from nests on the rocks above us. The light became dim and the temperature dropped into the 60's. Our GPS signal vanished. How would we know when we reached ground zero? My reading about the cache told me that many parties who find the cache send one geocacher to keep track of the GPS signal above while the others search below. We hadn't done that. We just kept hoping our GPS would get us close enough to look.

As it turned out, circumstances brought us to the right spot. Up ahead we could see a huge pile of rocks that blocked the canyon and there was only one way to follow the canyon. We had to climb over the pile. The unstable rocks moved under our feet as we climbed the heap of boulders, but when we reached the top everything looked very familiar to me. It looked like the setting where people had taken pictures of their find. We checked the GPS and thought we were close. We looked down the other side of the rock pile and decided we were better off staying right where we were. The descent looked risky. Climbing up is always easier than climbing down.

Step three, find the cache. A ten foot pile of rocks has hundreds, if not thousands, of hiding places. We began looking in all the nooks and crannies. We progressed to moving rocks and looking underneath. We didn't want to do too much rock moving, though. The more we moved rocks the more unstable the rock pile became. We checked the GPS to see if it still said we were in the right spot. We were.

I kept reminding myself that this was a 5/5. This was the hardest kind cache to find. It wasn't supposed to be easy. So I put my patience into overdrive and began analyzing my surroundings more carefully. I remembered the pictures I had seen of people stuck Winnie-the-Pooh-style into a hole. I didn't see a hole like that. Were we going to have to DNF our 1000th find? No way! I told myself we were not leaving without our signature in the logbook.

It doesn't take long on a search like this to decide that we had looked everywhere we could possibly look. There were just too many places, and we couldn't look in all of them.

TSPI stood up to get one more GPS reading. To get any reading at all we had to stand at the highest point of the rock pile and lift the GPS as high as we could. TSPI stood like the Statue of Liberty lifting her torch, waited for the GPS to update, lowered his hand, read the screen, and turned around to tell me there was no further information. Then his eyes fell at just the right angle to spot the cache. YES! The old only-visible-from-one-angle trick! He reached down into the hole and plucked the cache out. We signed the log making sure to note our 1000th milestone, and took pictures of the two of us holding up our milestone sign. The picture was an adventure all its own. Imagine setting the timer on the camera and then picking your way over loose boulders and sliding, smiling into place all within ten seconds. I'm surprised TSPI didn't break his leg.

When I replaced the cache I found the hiding spot was well below my feet. I almost had to get down on my belly for the Winnie the Pooh pose to put it back. I arranged the rocks like TSPI described and we celebrated all the way back to the car. I had hat hair all day long, but it didn't matter. We had conquered the 5/5! Driving down the moguls was a lot easier than climbing up them. The bumps and lurches felt more like celebratory leaps.

Next stop Yosemite!

# 15Tango's First Find

Matthew Mikesell
*15Tango*

I'm one of the geocaching old-timers. I read the
now famous 'Outside Magazine' article, and since I already had
a Garmin GPS II-plus that was gathering dust, I checked out the
geocaching website and became a user (with username
mwm15T – my initials and the MGRS grid-zone designator for
most of Minnesota) on 21 December 2000. My geocaching ID
number is 1252 (I believe new users get 8-digit ID numbers
now). I'm one of the first Premium Members, and since I
haven't let my membership lapse since that became available,
I'm still listed as a Charter Member.

When I first signed on, there were only a handful of caches
in Minnesota, and I didn't hide or seek anything right away. It
ended up on the back burner – I did lurk on the forums every
once in a while, and that was about it. One thing I remember
well in the time after I became a user and before I found my
first cache was checking the forum after 9/11, wondering if this
fledgling activity was done before it really got off the ground.

In late January 2002, my girlfriend and I were looking for

something different to do. She wasn't into skiing, and with a mild winter, skiing was pretty much a wash anyhow; we'd already seen the latest exhibits and Omni show at the Science Museum and were growing bored with bowling. I mentioned geocaching, and she agreed we should try it out. She also wanted to see Coldwater Spring. At the time, the land still belonged to the Bureau of Mines, and along with the spring, which is sacred to the areas Native Americans, there were old buildings that have been sitting abandoned for years.

The only time we could access the area was before 3pm during the week, so we planned a Friday afternoon expedition. Se we set out armed with my old GPS and a handful of printed cache pages, including the one for "Camp Coldwater Spring – GC1F01." When we got there, we first found a Hmong shrine in a hollow tree, but that was too far from the coordinates, so we followed the GPS to the side of a maintenance building, where we found a plastic pencil box, and lo and behold, that was the cache. Here is my first ever cache log –

"I've been on geocaching for a while, since I read the article in Outside magazine, but this is the first time I've gone seeking caches. Got to the place at around 2:30 with my girlfriend and cache partner--we also explored around the pond and looked at the shrines. Beautiful day for caching--it's hard to believe its January 25th in Minnesota. Lots of ducks on the pond. Thanks King Boreas for bringing us here, and we hope you're not too disappointed that winter is kind of a wash this year!!!"

That day, we managed to find two more geocaches before dark, driving many miles to just get three finds. And I was instantly hooked. The next day, I went out on my own (much to my girlfriend's chagrin) and found some more.

Now, over 14 years later, I'm still quite an active geocacher. I just bought my sixth GPS receiver. The GPS II-plus, while accurate, was pretty "stupid" – its map just showed a straight line between my location and my destination, and while it would save tracks, I needed to download them to my computer to see them on an actual map.

It got replaced by a Garmin eTrex Vista that actually had maps, but because the rubber band around the outside kept coming off, that gave way to a Garmin GPSmap 60CSx so I could have color maps and routing. Wanting the ability to load many more maps and geocaches, I had an Oregon for a while, until I accidentally left that on the roof of a car and drove off. I replaced the Oregon with a GPSmap 62st, but its rubber band practically disintegrated (I think I carried it too many times with bug spray on my hands, and then left it in the sun too long). And since I'm getting tired of replacing the Gorilla Tape that I use to replace the rubber band, I've now gone to a GPSmap 64s.

I've seen technology advance from printouts and hand-jamming coordinates to downloading a couple thousand geocaches with descriptions, logs, hints, and additional waypoints in a matter of seconds. But while the technology has advanced, geocaching still does the same thing it's always done for me over the years – it gets me outside and walking around, and even in the same area where I started, I'm still discovering something new all the time.

I currently have over 8,000 finds. I've found caches in 28 States, as well as Afghanistan, Kyrgyzstan, Kuwait, and Iraq. I even changed my username not long after I started, from mwm15T to 15Tango. But after all that, I'll still always remember my first cache find at Camp Coldwater Spring.

# *Arachnid Alley*
## *(Or How I Learned to Stop Screaming and Love the Spider)*

Stephen Mark Rainey
*Damned Rodan*

Since I was old enough to scream in terror, and for the better part of fifty-some years, I was the very definition of an Arachnophobe. It didn't matter whether the eight-legged crawly was big, brown, and hairy, or tiny, black, and smooth as onyx; if the two of us came to share a sphere of influence, one of us was going to die. Clearly, since I'm still around to write about such things, it was I who prevailed, though not at all times with nerves intact. Now, if spiders as a species should have long, empathic memories, then I fear my ultimate demise might prove unpleasant. But for the moment, let us let bygones be bygones, and focus on how my attitude toward multi-legged predatory critters came to make a dramatic shift.

I started Geocaching in 2008 and have been an addict ever since. It really wasn't until taking up caching, when I found myself ever more frequently trespassing into their environment, that I came to discover how ubiquitous our eight-legged friends really are. Here in North Carolina, black widows inhabit the dark spaces beneath every other rock, and multitudes of huge, hairy wolf spiders lurk in the woods, especially at night, coolly observing you with their clusters of green, glowing eyes. Every now and then, you run across some belligerent specimen that seems intent on reminding you of why your dread is anything but irrational. But most of the time, they're as anxious to get away from us big, lumbering behemoths as we are from them.

It was early summer, 2009. I had been Geocaching regularly for just over a year, with something like a thousand finds to my name. Here in the Piedmont Triad, we have a good number of caches placed in those claustrophobic places where the sun doesn't shine: down in the miles of lightless tunnels and culverts that run beneath the streets, businesses, and homes. There was one in particular that required spending a few hours underground — "Greensboro Underground" (GC1R7EV) — and having discovered the joys of claiming a numerous "extreme" caches, I took it to heart to go after it. A couple of other seasoned adventurers joined me on this endeavor, and for the purposes of this tale, I shall call them Bully Sneakdog and Night-Duck.

To let you know a little about my companions: Bully is not a small man, possessing a fairly rugged physique, relaxed demeanor, and a pointed sense of humor. Night-Duck is a respected — well, sort of — businessman in the community, but among geocachers, he's something of a legend. His finds number well into the five digits, and he hasn't missed a day of finding at least one cache in over nine years. I felt confident I was in good company to undertake this adventure, and I came prepared with ample headlamps and flashlights, extra batteries, waterproof boots, expendable clothes, and cautious optimism about finding the cache. I had gone short distances underground any number of times, but this was going to be a big one, and I surely didn't know quite what to expect.

There were several stages to the cache, the first being above ground and not all that difficult. From there, though, the coordinates led us to a spot along a stream underneath a bridge not far from my workplace. We wandered about for a while, trying to figure out just where we needed to go. At last, we saw it: a small opening in the bank on the other side of the creek, a concrete culvert, which we knew we had to enter. I confess it was a bit daunting, for while it was large enough to enter at a crouch, there was no end in sight. Just a wall of pure darkness beyond which our lights could not penetrate.

Bully bit the bullet and went in first. Night-Duck followed, and I played Tail-End Charlie, which, at the time, seemed the wisest place to be in case we had to make a sudden about-face and book on out of there. The most recent logs from just a few days before, indicated that hunters had encountered copperheads, which are about as common here as the black widows. Now, while my fear of spiders might have been extreme, I have never had any such fear of snakes, even the venomous variety. Still, I can't say I wanted to come upon one where my mobility was so limited. But on we pressed, and after a time, despite his size, Bully had put considerable distance between Night-Duck and me.

His voice echoed through the darkness: "There's a junction ahead!"

No sooner had he spoken when a blood-curdling scream rang through the enclosed space, piercing my eardrums like a steel spike. It went on for what seemed a mighty long time, and Night-Duck and I began to call after Bully, wondering what had happened. We feared he might have come upon a vertical shaft and fallen into it.

"Bully! Are you all right?"

"Jesus God!"

"What's the matter?"

"This is the biggest spider I've ever seen!"

"Seriously?"

"Oh, God. There's another one!"

Oh. No. Not spiders.

"THE PLACE IS FULL OF THEM!"

Night-Duck and I debated a moment. Up ahead, there were spiders. But there lay the stage we needed to claim this geocache. Well, we had our priorities, and so it was decided. The two of us wormed our way through the pipe until we reached the junction, where we came upon Bully cowering in a corner.

Oh, my lord.

The stone walls of that confined space were absolutely crawling with big, black, gray, and brown hairy spiders, the smallest of which probably had a four-inch leg span. Over one of the three openings in this chamber, the cache owner had painted a fluorescent arrow, which indicated the route to our destination. However, also above this opening hung a huge black spider, eyeing us with undisguised derision. Bully put his foot down and declared that he was not going into the pipe with that spider hanging there. So, feigning the air of the undaunted, I took my hiking stick and knocked the spider off the wall — at which point it began to scurry straight toward Bully.

Only if you have ever heard a scalded cat screaming in an enclosed, echoing chamber could you imagine the sound that Bully unleashed. Shrieking all the while, he began a dance routine that would have shamed Gene Kelly. Night-Duck and I could hardly refrain from chuckling, and then, before we knew it, we were both doubled over in the grip of uncontrollable laughter.

Finally, Bully came to his senses, and Night-Duck and I began to take stock of our situation. Indeed, spiders were everywhere, but they weren't doing anything. Just hanging about, minding their own business. We had come this far; we couldn't possibly turn and retreat now.

Night-Duck looked at me earnestly and pointed to the marked opening. Straight out of Indiana Jones, he said, "It could be dangerous. You go first."

Yep, that pipe was also full of spiders. But there was nothing for it but to go for broke. Then, as I ducked to make my way inside, something fell onto my shoulder with a distinctive plop.

"Mr. Duck, my friend," I said. "Please tell me that was a not a spider."

"Nope, just a hunk of grass from the drain up there."

"You wouldn't lie to me, would you?"

"Not about that."

All right then. On I went, past veritable walls of spiders

whose eyes followed me, all exuding menace. Yet, after Bully's dance-and-holler routine, I could not bring myself to be afraid. I found I was actually still chuckling.

I had reached a milestone in my life.

And from that moment on, Arachnophobia became a thing of the past. I knew that spiders had no desire to bother me. If anything, they were probably laughing at me. I'm pretty sure they were all laughing at Bully.

We went on to find that cache — several hours and innumerable pipes later. It was quite the experience in the underground, to be concluded with one more heartfelt chuckle.

Upon our egress, we popped out of a culvert that put us right on the sidewalk along a major thoroughfare. And wouldn't you know it, we emerged like muck-and-mud-covered phantoms before an elderly lady walking her poodle dog down the sidewalk. The lady let out a yelp, clearly not expecting to encounter anything quite as strange as the three of us.

In that moment, I was the spider.

And I've been laughing about it ever since.

# *Spider's Revenge*

LA Newell
*J&LA*

## This was my first brush with death.

Well, sorta.

The sun was hot and the sky clear, about 85° F. I drank a small amount of water before I left and grabbed a soda for J to give me afterward as my victory drink.

We'd scoped out the cache before and determined it would be better to come back with safety gear. Today we returned, hoping to finally conquer Amber's Revenge II (GCHRB3), which required traversing a huge erosion control barrier stuck in the bank of the Salt Creek in Lincoln, Nebraska. Made of large vertical I-beams and horizontal pieces of questionable lumber, the cache was an ammo can tied to the very top of the beam 4th from the end. Of course, nowhere in the rule book did it say this thing had to be plumb… and it wasn't. The entire structure leaned steeply toward the water to the south and to the east, and 2-3 of the beams nearest the cache were completely rusted out and hanging precariously at water level.

I'd hoped I could bypass the long shuffle across potentially rotting wood by sliding down the bank to the tiny island the ducks were sitting the last visit. But this time, due to recent downpours, the water was nearing flood stage, so my idea was no longer feasible. The island had been completely washed away.

Reluctantly, we went down the steep bank to where the structure was anchored, and started getting ready. I put on my harness and clipped two sections of webbing to it using carabineers, donned a pair of gloves to protect my hands from the sun-heated metal and splinters, and started pulling myself up. The second row from the top seemed the most comfortable, so I clipped my safety lines on and started inching along toward my goal. At every I-beam and obstruction, including annoying metal bars that didn't belong there, I had to use a lot of energy to pull myself around, hold on with one hand, move anchor points, and dodge a multitude of spiders.

About three-quarters of the way across, I began feeling ill. I was no longer sweating, but for me, that seemed pretty normal. Not sure if it was the heat, lack of breakfast, physical exhaustion or simple dehydration, but regardless, I was determined to make it to this cache. I'm not terribly afraid of heights, but it was surreal watching the rapid, swollen river rushing briskly below me, splashing against the beams like a mad toddler. If I was going to fall, chances are I would be washed away.

I eventually worked my way to the ammo can, taking care to avoid the numerous mushy spots in the wood. At the cache, I rested for a few moments, then lifted the container only to see something large and black fall from behind it. I assumed it was another spider. I flicked a small one off of me - then opened the cache. Inside was a nice collection of toys, probably a trackable or two, and a large notebook. The comments in it were actually very funny. I read them all, then added something about really wanting a helicopter, and how I wished I had a can of Raid®, because all arachnids are my arch enemies.

Just as I went to close the cache, I was attacked on the hand by a larger Wolf Spider, about the size of a half-dollar. In a single motion, I smacked it into the container then closed the lid. I sniggered maniacally to myself, "There, another travel bug for the next visitor, hahaha!"

Then, only seconds later, like an evil shadow lurking in the corner of my eye, I noticed something black on the back of my right thigh. OMG!!! I seriously thought it was a bird. Nope, turns out it was a huge dark brown spider - not exaggerating - the size of my entire hand! I recoiled, thankful that I was wearing a harness to keep me from falling. I immediately swept it off. It made a thud when I smacked into its disgusting giant body, followed by a satisfying sploosh as it hit the water below. J was up on the sidewalk by now, a solid 60 feet from the water, and he had the camera. After I repeated several times, "Look in the water at the big spider!" he finally gasped as he spotted it. He was able to get a clear photo without a long telephoto lens. All I know is it was "Bigger than I care to remember... lives in the same state as me." Ugh! I echoed this exact sentiment in my log.

After all this excitement, I was feeling very faint, yet I knew I still had to return to safety. I replaced the cache and started inching my way across, getting sicker and weaker at every metal beam. I assumed the combined stress of the elements was wearing me down. I knew if I were to pass out, I would at least be tied onto the structure by my anchors, but I also knew a rescue squad would have an easier time getting to me if I was lower. So I started dropping myself down a row after every few sections, eventually coming to a dead standstill about 8 feet from a small, precarious strip of land. I was unable to move any further.

Everything was going black, I could no longer hear anything, and I was losing consciousness with no hope of recovery. Soon, an ambulance would have to be called to my rescue. Luckily, J still had my celebratory pop in his possession and was able to work his way to where he could just barely get the bottle into my hand. We figured it wasn't the best choice but better than nothing, so I chugged it all. About 5 minutes of hanging there on the verge of blacking out, I started to rouse a little bit. It still took another 10 minutes for me to work my way down and over to where J was. He half-dragged me up the embankment to where I had entered, refusing to let me lay down in the grass... or up on the sidewalk... or along the trail. He half-carried me to a nearby table behind a business where I plopped down in exhaustion while he went for the car and our cooler. Another hour later, after LOTS of water, air conditioning and a good meal, I was ready to move on.

Another awesome find, and a favorite point awarded!

# *A Day on the Lake*

Emily Albers
*Stardust2018*

We arrived at Winton Woods Park on a nice, sunny morning. The birds were chirping, bugs buzzing, and the heat of the sun with a cool breeze made it a great day for caching. Lots of people were enjoying one of the last warm days before a chilling fall.

Our group of six, including two friendly muggles, was ready for a day of caching adventures. Our mission was to find our first paddle cache. We rented canoes from the boathouse and pushed off shore into the lake to begin our journey.

We started with the closest cache on the map. The short trip to ground zero was smooth and filled with picture taking. As we came up to the bank, I immediately saw it hanging so we glided the canoe under the cache to claim it. Cautiously, we brought it down to sign and unscrewed the lid. Nobody wanted to drop it into the lake. We passed it around from one boat to the other and snuck it back into the trees.

We were so excited! We had just found our first paddle cache! Locking our sights on the next few caches, we headed out. Most of them were similar: a container hanging in a tree overlooking the vast water.

One geocache led us to what seemed to be the middle of the lake or under the bridge going over the lake. We weren't exactly sure where to look since the coordinates weren't very clear. We tried to use our geosense for this one, but unfortunately, we could not find it.

We moved on to the next cache. This cache was actually placed on the bank of the lake in the midst of tree roots, instead of in the tree's leaves. I couldn't reach it from the canoes, but I could definitely see it. Finally one of our friendly muggles climbed out of the front of the boat onto shore and snagged it. Took us a minute to figure out how to get it back to the boats until I thought of using the oar. So we extended the oar and it safely made it back for us to sign. When we were finished, the cache was then sent back to its original hiding spot.

After everyone was back in the canoes we pushed off towards yet another cache. This one was again in a tree. At the last few caches we had been noticing that some of the trees had these unique brownish, blackish, spiders everywhere. They would get into the boats and scare the people in the group who are afraid of spiders.

At this particular cache, as one of us was getting the cache down a spider had dropped out of the tree and somehow fell into his mouth. All he could say right after that happened was "I swallowed it."

We all busted out laughing! We decided to make that our last cache because it was pretty late into the afternoon by now. As we journeyed back, we saw many people on paddle boats, canoes, and kayaks. There was a very nice man who was paddle boarding with his dog. The little fluffy white dog was too cute, and seemed to be having a great time on the peaceful waters.

Paddling and paddling, we made it back to the bridge, where we couldn't find a cache. We looked around a little more and still had no idea where it could be. After a bit, we saw there was another cache nearby that we hadn't searched for yet. Our eyes were instantaneously magnetized to it as we paddled up to it. We signed the log and hid it back among the deep green leaves.

As we went to leave, both canoes got stuck in the shallow

water near the bank. Finally we wiggled one boat free, and then the other, but we weren't let off the hook yet. One of our boats then got caught on a sand bar. Before getting free, a picture was taken and posted with the caption "Stuck on a sand bar" because we all thought it was funny.

As we got closer to shore and somebody remembers their selfie stick! We got our canoes as close to each other as possible and figured out how we were going to pull this off without dropping a phone in the water. There were many failed attempts that were blurry, someone wasn't ready, or it just didn't work. Finally we got the perfect picture. It captured the whole day of fun and adventure.

It was the perfect day with friends and family doing something we all love.

# Vegas: Nothing but Trouble

Aaron Hobson
*Fugads*

I was in Las Vegas – right on the strip - for business. It was my first time spending time in Sin City, and I found the strip appalling. Glitzy entertainment is just not my thing. But finding grimy urban caches in the ghettos bordering the strip… well, that sounded fun!

If only the company had provided me a rental car, things might have turned out differently. With wheels, I could have driven out to the edges of town, and found some truly awesome caches scrambling through the Red Rocks. But since the Casino that hosted the conference had a free shuttle to the airport, I didn't get a car. But that wasn't going to stop me. I was determined to have a good time, as only a geocacher could. So each morning I'd get up early, pull on my running kit and take to the strip before most Las Vegas revelers would even consider getting up.

The first couple days, I plied the strip, which was amusing in a freakish kind of way. After a few days, I craved something different, so I started looking toward caches out in the "hoods." Most caches out in the periphery of the strip were pretty standard stuff, but there was one that really stood out.

GC2Y1XF, DGS Sign of a Dirtbag, was the diamond in the rough, at least by my thinking. It is one of those Urban T4 caches that takes you deep into concrete drain and sewer systems. I hadn't done one of these before, but I'm an adventurous type, and this cache called to me like none other.

So, a few days into the conference, after my work commitments, I geared up for the 3+ mile (uninspiring) jog out to this particular cache. On the way, I stopped only for a few lackluster hides in parking lots. At GZ, I located the cache quickly from above. Then, all I needed to do was find a subterranean passage which would allow me to lay hands on the logbook. This is where things went horribly wrong.

You see, I cache with a Garmin GPSmap 60CSx, a great device, but it doesn't support paperless caching (and no I didn't have a smartphone either). So when I'm going somewhere, I try to read up on the caches that look good, and then I load up a bunch of waypoints and just kind of hope for the best. You might call this "old-school style" cacheing: no hints, no reading last logs, no reading cache descriptions. I just get to the coords and attempt to make a find. What I was missing on this specific day in Vegas was a way-point for a suggested parking area 1/4 mile to the west. Instead of heading in that direction, I made the classic geocacher blunder and took the straight line approach to the canal that was just visible to the north.

I hit the flood canal, scrambled down and immediately started looking for a storm-drain entrance. I found one quickly, and it appeared to be heading directly toward the cache. So far so good, right? But it was a ridiculously small space - maybe 24" diameter. Standing there, trying to work up the nerve to crawl in, I almost convinced myself that there was no way this was the correct entrance. But I stifled the fear, and decided to crawl in and check things out. Since I was only wearing running shorts, a t-shirt, and a hydration pack, the hands-and-knees crawling through the concrete tube was rather painful.

I had a small flashlight clutched in one hand, and with my other hand, I frantically tried to clear the cobwebs. It was miserable! After about 30ft or so, I reached a turnaround point:

a junction between two tube sections. I crouched low, out of my supine position, to stretch. I absolutely could have turned around there. But I didn't. Instead, I looked down the next section of tube, and I saw another junction about 100ft further. I sucked in a deep breath, and got back down on my hands and knees.

I crawled over a dead, desiccated bird. The spider webs ceased to be as thick the deeper and darker I went. All I could think about the entire time is how I better find that cache.

I finally reached the next junction, and once again, was confronted with another long passage going off in a slightly different direction. It looked to be about another 200 ft or so, and it was seriously dark and foreboding. Despite the growing pain in my hands and knees, I continued.

"I must get this cache, I must get this cache" ... repeating it over and over in my head.

I was already composing my found log in my head. The minutes felt like hours as I wriggled and squirmed one painful foot at a time.

Finally, I was at the terminal junction. I was able to stand in a little alcove where storm-water would normally drain off the street. I could see car tires fly by just inches from my head. I quickly scanned the area ... no cache. It just looked ... wrong.

It slowly dawned on me that I was in the incorrect storm drain. I stuck my GPS out of the opening of the drain and waited for it to locate satellites. What I wouldn't have given to be a pedestrian on the street right then, witnessing a bloody hand reach out of the storm-drain clutching an electronic device!

After a minute, I pulled the device in and took a look. It said the cache was another 0.2 miles away! I was definitely, definitely in the wrong place. I wanted morphing powers - to just morph and squeeze right out of the storm grate. I desperately wanted out. My body was aching and trembling from the exertion of pulling myself through the tiny, rough tube. And there I sat, sunlight bouncing through the grating above my head, staring at the gaping concrete maw of the tube I had just crawled through. I had no choice. I had to get out. I sucked down some water, took a few deep calming breaths, and then inserted my body (very much against its will) back into the misery.

Going out was twice as agonizing as coming in. My elbows and knees were already raw and bloody, and protested each movement. At several points I stopped in near defeat, my body collapsing to the floor of the tube, heaving and cramped. My muscles felt like they were giving way, but all I could do was grit my teeth and keep going.

An eternity passed.

I thought about how stupid I was to come in the first place. Chasing a geocache! Doomsday scenarios pass through my head: Man Found Dead in Storm Drain: treasure hunt under Las Vegas goes bad.

I shook the morbid thoughts loose and kept going. Finally, I emerged from the wall of the flood canal, gasping for air and trembling all over. For 10 minutes or so I just sat there, sucking the remaining water from my pack. Thinking about having to jog 3+ miles back to the hotel was depressing, to say the least. My water was out, and I hadn't brought money.

But I was out! I held back joyful tears.

I got up, and meandered west up the canal looking for an easier way to climb out. My muscles were so cramped and spasmodic that I couldn't climb up what only shortly before was practically effortless. I was a staggering wreck.

A quarter mile or so up the canal, I spotted a ladder leading out of the canal, and another storm drain, this one much bigger. Could this be the right way to the geocache, I wondered? It looked like a walk in the park in comparison to what I had just been through. Ragged as I was, I actually approached this new entrance, thinking maybe I would check it out too. But then I heard some babbling noises coming out of the entrance, and I stopped in my tracks. To this day, I don't know if it was some hobo camped out in the drain, or my subconscious creating a hallucination in order to keep me out. I backed off and turned to the nearby ladder. Forcing my aching body up it, I got back onto the street and then commanded my legs to start trotting.

The next day was the last day of the conference. I must have looked dreadful, because several people asked if I was ok. A long-sleeved shirt would have been nice, to hide the massive scabs on my elbows, but I hadn't brought one. But the sidelong glances from the conference attendees was nothing compared to the hell I got from my wife when she found out what I had done. Let's just say I had my caching privileges revoked after this mishap. But on the plus side, this was my best DNF ever!

# *Streaking Through Romania*

Dave Hickman II
*OrigamiFolder*

In the winter of 2013, my wife and I took a trip to visit her family in Romania. I spoke to my brother-in-law Bogdan ahead of time, as he was the only member of the family in Râmnicu Sărat with a car and I was in the middle of my 500 day caching streak at the time, and I knew I'd need transportation. My wife's home town is rather small and had absolutely no geocaches whatsoever, but some of the larger cities, surrounding countryside and naturally the capital (Bucharest) did. He was gracious, and fascinated with my stories of caching in the US, so he agreed to take me out and see if we could uncover some.

I am from Kansas City, Missouri, and we have a lot of high-quality geocaches, but our understanding of terrain ratings varies greatly from the fine folks in Romania. The first cache we attempted was on the outskirts of this town where you had to park near an old soviet era bridge that spanned the Buzău River and was closed to anything but pedestrian traffic. We walked to the edge of the bridge, and my wife and her sister wished us luck as we slowly walked/slid down the side of it, about 50 feet to the frozen tundra-like shore below. It was blistery and -15°C (4°F), so we were wearing several layers of clothing, but you could still feel the wind whip across the mixture of frozen ice and water. I pulled out my trusty GPS, and cautiously, we stomped through the snow which was several feet deep in places, thanks to drifts.

As I got closer to the GZ, I noticed the coordinates were pointing us into a large collection of bramble bushes. We cautiously tiptoed in and around them, but despite our best efforts, the thorns kept catching our clothes. Then, after one poorly-placed step backward, one of the thorns pierced through the bottom of my boot and into my foot! After a good 20 minute search (and a pause to dislodge the thorn in my foot), we decided Mother Nature had won this round, and retreated back to the warmth of the car. So much work for a DNF and that was a 2-star terrain cache!

Obviously skeptical, the new cachers questioned our next destination. I wanted to keep them interested (and warm) so we ventured into town to search for what the cache page assured us was an "easy" cache. It turned out to be a nano on a massive statue in front of city hall. When we arrived, the weather had caused the muggle factor to drop to zero. The design of the statue allowed for many hiding spots though, and after 20 minutes of searching, our 4 sets of eyes still hadn't found it. At this point, a local policeman showed up, and it was no surprise when he said he had never heard of Geocaching before. He also mentioned his concern about our loitering and intense interest in the statue in front of a government building. Luckily, my native speaking partners were able to calm his concerns, and so as to not push our luck, we headed off once again.

I was really starting to worry that my streak would come to an end there in Romania, 5,000 miles from home. But as luck would have it, this town's "city park" housed one more hopeful find. Based on my previous observations, I expected the park to be a few blocks long and situated between some towering, concrete apartment buildings. What it actually turned out to be was a healthy-sized nature preserve with long trails and a lake, right alongside a Federal "military zone."

Well, Geocachers are persistent, if nothing else, so with my somewhat-reluctant family members in tow, we parked and geared up for adventure. As we exited the car, my sister-in-law walked to the edge of the woods and snapped a few branches off of the nearby trees. She handed each of us a branch. I thanked her for the walking stick, and she explained it was far more important than that.

Apparently, Romania is home to large packs of wild dogs, and it's best to be ready to defend oneself, should you encounter one. A little concerned, but bolstered by their apparent lack of fear, we ventured deep into the snow-covered woods.

Stopping every couple hundred feet to check our bearing and scout for dogs, we trekked deeper and deeper into the trees until I felt a hand on my shoulder urging me down. I kneeled in place and looked back to see Bogdan pointing at a deer racing into the clearing ahead, followed by 20 dogs of various sizes. As the deer disappeared beyond the thick woods, the faster dogs kept chase, and the small, slower ones stopped and wandered around briefly. I was concerned they would come our way, and saw that I was not alone as everyone around me readied their sticks. The alpha dogs must have succeeded, however, because the rest of the pack ran off in that same direction a short time later.

Another quarter of a mile in, and we had arrived at the GZ. Thanks to experience, I zeroed right in on a likely spot, but it was a hollow stump filled with several inches of ice. We chipped and scraped until finally, I laid eyes on one of the most beautiful geocaches I'd ever visited! The container was just a flimsy piece of cracked plastic, but by goodness it was a hard-fought win! After signing our names and leaving one of my trademark origami cranes, we cautiously returned as conquering heroes.

…and that was just day one of the trip!

# Dobro pozhalovat' v Rossiyu, Welcome to Russia

Jessie Maxwell
*jtcoffee*

Here in Seattle, Washington, geocachers come from
all over the globe to experience the wonder of our landmarks,
our natural features, the Fremont Troll, and geocaching
headquarters located in none other than the Center of the
Universe. Visitors to Seattle often host short meet-and-greet
style events to introduce themselves to the locals and to
solidify, if all else fails, the coveted Washington State souvenir.
When I learned that my muggle husband and I would be
traveling to Moscow, Russia, in the fall of 2015, visions of
what my maps and graphs on my geocaching statistics page
would look like filled my mind.

I knew I had to get at least one cache in Russia while I was
visiting, but since I don't normally cache with a GPS unit, I
would have to figure out saving caches, wifi hotspots, global
data plans, and plug-in converters for my smartphone in order
to cache like I normally do in the States. I learned long ago not
to put all your eggs in one technology-basket (too many times

I've been on top of a mountain with no 4G) so I knew I had to create a failsafe plan to ensure I could get a cache in Russia.

This meant hosting an event.

When our plane tickets were acquired, I imagined meeting Russian geocachers and chatting over coffee. I submitted my event right away.

At this point in my caching career, I had never held an event, so I decided to hold a few preparatory events just so I could get into the swing of things. After one event down the street from my house and one in London on our way to Moscow, I was more than confident with my event-holding prowess.

And suddenly the 'will-attends' started rolling in! To my excitement, this event was becoming a reality. I started telling my friends and family (nearly all non-cachers) about my plans. Nearly all of them responded with questions like "Are you sure everyone there will speak English?" "What if no one shows up?" "What if a ton of people show up?" and "Aren't you nervous about having lunch with a bunch of people you don't know?"

I laughed them off – people have events in foreign countries all the time. Most of my 'will-attends' were in English and the location had been recommended by a local cacher. This event in Moscow would be no different.

I hoarded trackables to take on my trip like a squirrel collecting nuts. Armed with my own trackables, things to trade, pathtags as gifts, and a fresh new event log, we took off on our multi-stop trip that would end in Moscow. As we went through security just before we crossed the pond, I looked up toward the line of luggage and saw an officer with my suitcase.

"Is this one yours?" She asked me.

I told her it was. She had me follow her since she had to look through it. I took the 20 foot walk-of-shame over to the small table where soon many of my belongings would be strewn. My husband had gathered the rest of our things and joined us with a smirk. If ever either of the two of us had an issue in security, it was usually me. Last time it was my water bottle, which I didn't bring this time, so what was it?

The officer was still prodding and moving things around in my bag, when she said, "The scan showed a large mass of metal or something in here…" and then she pulled my little trackable bag out into the open.

I knew at once what had piqued their interest. I started to smile and looked over at my husband, who also recognized the little bag and had started shaking his head. As I looked back over, the officer had the little bag open and was reaching inside. Somehow, all of the trackables and their various attachments of key chains, toys, and other baubles had become a veritable bird's nest, tangled together in a mass that cascaded down about a foot from her gingerly pinched fingers, jingling like a tiny wind chime.

As I chuckled at this mess, I quickly offered the explanation of "They're game pieces! Tokens in a game I play with friends.,"

I was hoping that was specific-yet-vague enough to calm her fears and let us move on. I had tried to explain geocaching to Border Patrol once before on my first caching trip to Canada, and that quickly went downhill when geocaching was described as "looking for boxes all over the world with nothing in them."

I figured in this case, less detail was better. She smiled, nodded, and put everything back and sent us on our way. It was smooth sailing from there, except for my husband making cracks that geocaching might have prevented him from attending his seminars.

When we arrived in Moscow, we spent our time with my husband's collaborators: students and professors at the University. They had heard I had some sort of meeting planned toward the end of my trip but they wanted to know who these people were and how had I found them without ever being in Moscow?

I tried to explain first what geocaching was, and then what an event cache was, and how I knew who was coming even though I'd never met them before. They asked me questions if I was sure they could speak English, if I knew how many exactly were coming, and if I knew I could get myself from the university to the coffee shop using the subway on my own.

When 'no' was all I could answer to these questions, I was starting to question my good judgement. But I knew I had a couple of days – of course I could figure things out by then!

On the day of my event, traveling was no sweat. (I even picked up a find on my way there!) Ordering coffee and a sandwich was a challenge but worked out just fine. I settled in, pulled out my trackables and logbook, and began enjoying my lunch. About 20 minutes before the event officially began, that hot-cold panic set in after the what-ifs started rolling through my head:

What if no one shows up?

What if a ton of people show up?

What if no one speaks English?

What on earth was I thinking holding an event in a place I'd never been, in a country where I don't speak more than "hello" and "thank you" in the language?

A seemingly infinite number of scenarios went through my head ranging from possible to absurd… when suddenly my attendees started to arrive. All of the fear melted away and we had a fun, memorable time – just like I'd hoped. We navigated conversations, traded trackables, shared stores of near-misses with police, and gave recommendations for the caches I should find with the rest of my time

I would recommend all geocachers who travel to new places to hold an event when you get there. Just make sure you put those trackables in your checked luggage!

# My First Cache, Namibia-style

Judy Nyman-Schaaf
*duma332*

Isn't it funny how sometimes a single thing or event occurs that you weren't expecting in the least and it can become an important part of your life?

My husband and I went on a much-anticipated trip to Namibia and Botswana in 2010 and although it was a fabulous trip in every possible way, the one thing that has had the most impact on me wasn't on the itinerary. I was introduced to geocaching; which has now become a very significant part of my life.

This African adventure was with only two other couples so we were all traveling in one vehicle. Our guide, Gavin, aka Team GBS, asked if any of us geocached. No one knew anything about it and I had only vaguely heard of it – which is pretty unbelievable considering I actually live in Seattle, two miles away from Geocaching Headquarters! I had to travel 9,500 miles to Namibia to learn about geocaching and become hooked.

As Gavin, an avid geocacher, was explaining it to us, the others showed little or no interest, but I was intrigued. He said we would be traveling near seven geocaches on our trip and he would stop if any of us wanted him to. I liked the idea of geocaching taking us to places of interest. Gavin, who had been a guide for years, said he discovered new areas to show tourists because caching took him there. For instance, there is a cache by a huge pit in the ground where bats live and come out at night (GCK8ZJ, Wondergat). Bats are fascinating to watch and he didn't know about it before caching.

On our first morning, as we headed from Windhoek to the coast, we were going to be driving by the first geocache. I was excited to experience my first geocaching adventure and to actually see what it was all about; I learn more by doing rather than just hearing or reading about things. At the time, Gavin only had his GPS from his small airplane to use. He thrust it into my hands and told me to let him know when we were close. It was large and clunky and something I had never seen before, let alone understood.

He said a "regular" GPS would be more accurate because when you're in a plane needing to find an airport or landing strip, the GPS doesn't have to be very precise since it's really hard to miss an airport or landing strip once you're somewhat close. I'm technologically challenged so I was confused when I was trying to read it. We had only been in Africa two days and I was still jet-lagged and it was hot. At least those are the excuses I was using. Obviously, Gavin had been there before (after all, there aren't that many geocaches in Namibia!) so he knew when to pull over and stop, even without my help.

The cache was GCVGEN, Kuiseb Canyon Cache, on the banks of the Kuiseb River. Before our journey, when he had access to a printer, Gavin made copies of all the cache pages we would be passing along the way, just in case any of us were interested. He handed me the one for Kuiseb and had me decipher the hint manually because it was still encrypted. It took me a while since it was a long hint and I was unfamiliar with the process.

It read: "Hidden inside a hole in a rock with the entrance covered with loose stones." Loose stones?! There were loose stones everywhere but it did sound pretty interesting to me! I certainly wasn't dressed to be out traipsing in the countryside looking for a geocache; I thought I'd just be riding in the vehicle all day. Luckily, the sandals I had on were fairly substantial and not the flip flops I almost chose to wear so I wasn't too worried about spraining my ankle. And that was one of my first lessons – always wear appropriate clothing, especially shoes, when going geocaching.

Because it was really hot, my husband stayed under the bridge; the only shade near the vehicle. I was looking forward to a little walk to stretch my legs since I had been inactive for a couple of days with the long flights to Africa. However, that quickly wore off as we walked in oppressive heat on rocky ground. A couple of others started out with us on our trek down the dry riverbed but when we had to start climbing up a relatively steep slope on the bank, they fell back, so only Gavin and I hiked up.

Did I mention it was hot?

There was no shade anywhere and it was dusty in the arid landscape. I still had no clue what we were really doing, although Gavin was trying to get me to understand what the GPS was saying. We continued clambering up the steep hill; the loose rocks and my inappropriate footwear making it hard to climb. I was beginning to question just what the heck I was doing and perhaps my husband had the right idea by staying with the vehicle. But the anticipation of finding the cache kept me going.

I was curious what made Gavin so interested in this hobby, sport, or whatever it was called. Finally he stopped (even though my reading of the GPS still said something like 40 feet away) and started removing large loose rocks from an indentation in the hillside, revealing a hole hiding a lunch-box-sized container holding a log and several trinkets. At that moment I forgot about being hot and dusty! I was seduced by the thrill of the hunt and the joy of the find! Never before, or since, has a box full of inexpensive toys and useless items seemed so attractive to me!

You always remember your first!

The hike back to the vehicle seemed much shorter than the

way to the cache as I talked excitedly with Gavin about my first geocaching experience. As I arrived back to the others, tired and sweaty, they couldn't quite understand my enthusiasm. A few eyes glazed over as I bubbled on about it, but that was okay – that certainly isn't the only time people have looked that way when I talk about finding a cache! I couldn't wait until we searched for the next one.

We looked for the other six geocaches as our journey continued. We had one DNF so I experienced that disappointment; Gavin thought baboons found and destroyed the cache – not something you run into every day!

At the last one we found, I even took a TB whose mission is to travel the world. That's when I promised Gavin I would get my own GPS and place it in a Seattle cache within two weeks. That was over 3,000 caches ago. I will never forget Gavin for introducing me to the world of geocaching, making my life so much richer – and I will never forget that first geocache I "found".

# *Trovato*

John Dwyer
*Dwyers5*


It was late in the afternoon, on an otherwise unremarkable Thursday, when my boss stopped by my cubicle.

"You're going," he said.

I tried to suppress a smile and thanked him. This was going to be a great conference because there would be lots of interesting science and the ability to make great connections. The real reason I was smiling, however, was that it would be my first chance to Geocache in Florence, Italy.

The conference was pretty intense. After my arrival, it consisted of long days of talks and networking, followed by nights of socializing. I was really looking forward to day three of the conference because the talks scheduled that afternoon were totally irrelevant, and that was when I was going to finally do some Geocaching. I had spent many hours researching caches in the area, and many of them looked interesting. A couple of them had a lot of favorite points, so I decided that I would focus on those, including a multi cache at the Piazzale Michelangelo.

I did not have a car, so I walked from my hotel near the

Duomo and picked up a few caches as I made my way to the Old Bridge over the Arno River. The history here was unbelievable and it was a major distraction from my geocaching activities. I couldn't help but imagine a young lad searching for a cache Galileo had hidden along the river bank centuries ago.

"Walk 50 paces from the path toward the Arno," my imaginary lad said to his girlfriend. She rolled her eyes and followed. "Align the tree with Giovanni's butcher shop on the Old Bridge and then walk five paces. The cache is a clay pot in a cave by the bank."

"This is the last one we are doing, right?" the girlfriend asked. Ah, some things have never changed!

Once I was across the river, I made my way up the steep grade to the piazzale. It was basically a parking lot, with food and gift vendors circled around one of the many copies of the Michelangelo. The first waypoint of the multicache was here, and so I gathered the information and was ready to move on. I noticed, though, that there were many dozens of people milling around. Some of them had extremely expensive cameras mounted on tripods. These were not the type of folks who randomly hung out in parking lots, so I figured something big was about to happen. The photographers seemed relaxed, so I bought a Peroni from a cart vendor and hung around as more and more tourists piled into the parking lot.

"What's happening?" I asked a cute, young Italian girl who was there with her boyfriend.

"Eh, you don't know?" she replied in broken English. I shook my head. "Very beautiful," she replied, pointing to the city.

After about 15 minutes, there was a ripple of excitement within the crowd and I heard the clicking of cameras. I found a spot near the edge of the parking lot and viewed what was quite possibly the most amazing sight I had ever seen.

The Duomo was lit up in a brilliant orange hue, as if the sky had poured golden paint directly into the Arno. You see these types of pictures on postcards, but I couldn't believe I was seeing it for real. I took in the incredible view and snapped a few pictures myself. However, the gorgeous sunset also reminded me that I did not have much time to finish this multi cache before dark. I chugged my Peroni and input the coordinates for the next waypoint.

I wound up near an amazingly beautiful church, the San Miniato al Monte. It was still pretty light out, and the marble façade of the church was set in the same brilliant light as the city. Climbing the stairs and entering the cemetery, it was amazing how beautiful the view was for the people buried here. The creator of Pinocchio, Carlo Lorenzini, was in there someplace but I would have to look for that little treasure later. Eventually, I acquired enough information to assemble the final coordinates. The first set seemed way off, so I went back to the front of the church and double checked my math, and also read some previous logs. I eventually got a set of coordinates I felt comfortable with, and it looked like the cache was located somewhere behind the church. It was late dusk at this point but I ventured off and eventually found a path to a road that led to the rear of the church. The arrow on my GPS pointed me down a grassy, tree-lined path and I followed it into the growing darkness. When I was within 100 feet, it was clear I needed to be by the back wall of the church, and I as I carefully walked through the rocks and thick grass, I became nervous. There was an old backpack, torn apart with contents spilled out and a weather-worn wallet nearby. Obviously, this was a place pick-pockets came to explore their spoils. As a foreigner, with only the light from my phone flashlight to guide me, I suddenly felt vulnerable.

I finally arrived where the cache was hidden and began my search. The container was listed as a small, and many trackables had been passed through here, so I figured it had to be a reasonably-sized cache. The only place that could have hidden such a cache was somewhere along the wall. The wall was made of large stone bricks which were covered with green moss. Thick vines ran up the wall in places, so it was difficult to illuminate much with my feeble phone flashlight. The GPS was acting wonky, which only served to increase the creepy factor. I searched back and forth a few times, but kept returning to a place with a large crack in the wall. I removed a couple of loose rocks and was greeted with a shaft of light that came from inside the church. I could hear music, and chanting, and then I noticed the strong smell of incense. Some sort of ceremony was happening just on the other side of the wall. I couldn't see it, because the wall was so thick, but the crack was big enough to tease me with what was happening inside. It was a humbling moment, and again I thought of all the people who had prayed inside those walls and those who had stood where I now crouched. Looking around, I also wondered how many ghosts from the cemetery float over to haunt unsuspecting Geocachers.

"C'mon! I can't leave without finding this cache," I whispered. "Not after all this!"

I gently searched the sacred wall while trying to both ignore and take in all the unbelievable stuff going on around me. Then, in a small alcove within the 1000 year old foundation of this spectacular church, I spotted a plastic container.

"Trovato!" I said. I had seen that word on many Italian Geocache logs, and now I could claim that I, too, had found this incredible cache. Although it would never be recorded, I felt like for a moment I became a tiny part of the history of this building. I took my time signing the log and tried to cling to the thrill of the find as long as I could. This cache would definitely get a favorite point, but both it and the adventure that afternoon in Florence were unforgettable.

# Totally Amazing Geo-Race

Maude Stephany
*Family Extremes*

August 22, 2009 is a date that will linger in my memory for many years to come. Up until that time, our family had attended small caching events, CITO's and meetups in local restaurants. But on this day, we experienced a caching event that remains our favorite large Geocaching group event.

The Amazing Geo-Race was modeled after the popular television show The Amazing Race. It was filled with obstacles, challenges, as well as Temptations to lure you off the path, and one step further from winning. Our family was primed and ready to compete as the dynamic team of Family Extremes, comprised of Cacheman (my husband), Erised (our 14 year old son), Incogneat-oh (our 7 year old daughter), and me – StealthMaude.

As we approached the starting location, we saw a hoard of cachers collecting around a picnic table. We signed into the log book, and got the sheet with the coordinates for the "Temptation caches" that had been placed and waited. Just as we were getting settled and entering the coordinates into our GPS and Nuvi, Megaphone in hand, Teddy2K instructed us on the rules of the game. Then, he blew his whistle, and was almost mown down by the stampede of eager cachers. Our son leapt to the chase and obtained our first challenge: to find the dates on the statues in Historic Fort Langley BC.

The small town suddenly was swarming with Geocachers. There was a buzz of activity and chaos as we tried to follow Erised in our car, while he ran around on foot. Finally, we caught up with each other, he hopped into our Matrixmobile, and off we went.

We soon arrived at the first challenge, where we had to decide which activity we would participate in. Would we wait to receive a 20-minute chair massage, or participate in cardio boot camp? While it was tempting to start our day off in a leisurely way, we wanted a chance to win. StealthMaude puffed and panted along through 20 minutes of grueling boot camp. As soon as I was done, we ran toward the car and were off to our next set of coordinates.

They led us to a nearby bowling alley, where our mission was to get a strike. Cacheman flexed his arms, puffed out his chest, picked up a ball, and sent it hurtling down the alley. We watched as it travelled, seeming to swing to one side or the other. When it reached the pins, they fell like dominoes … all but one wobbly pin. We held our breath as we watched it unsure what would happen, then saw it tip slowly down. A strike! We collected our new coordinates and made a clean getaway.

Next, we arrived at a large park in the middle of Abbotsford, BC, which is full of bridges over water. First we tried to find a place to park, then hunted to find the best way to the cache. Finally, we found a Sudoku puzzle. Now Erised and StealthMaude teamed up to quickly solve it, so that we could discover the coordinates to our next destination.

We scrambled to the car again, but Incogneat-oh was getting anxious. She wanted to do the next challenge no matter what. It was almost lunch time when we pulled up to a well-known wings restaurant. Immediately, Incogneat-oh seemed to sense that food was involved. "I'll do it," she insisted.

"What are we doing here?" I asked the waitress.

"You have to eat 5 suicide hot wings," she said as she placed a plate of glistening bright red chicken wings before us.

"I'll do it," Incogneat-oh insisted. I looked at Cacheman doubtfully.

"Taste it first," the waitress suggested. Incogneat-oh dipped her finger in the sauce and shoved it in her mouth. She looked at Cacheman, tears streaming down her face. "You do it."

Cacheman swiftly ate the wings; we snatched up the coordinates for our next location, and headed toward the car. Then, looking at Cacheman, I noticed something. His face bloomed red, then purple. He poured one package of peanuts after another in his mouth. Meanwhile, Incogneat-oh wailed "I'm hungry and he's eating all my peanuts!" After promises that we would stop soon for something for lunch, we set out for our next location.

We travelled north and west, zipping through the highway traffic to Bridal Falls, BC. We arrived at the water slides, where one member of our team had to dare to take the completely dark Black Hole Slide, or face a penalty. Erised sprinted to the top while we waited below, and ordered some lunch. As soon as he emerged from the swirling darkness, we handed him a towel, piled into the car, and drove on to our next destination.

By now, Incogneat-oh was angry. She desperately wanted to do something. Besides, according to the rules, we HAD to let her do something or we would forfeit. So when our next task was to sink a golf ball at a nearby mini golf course, we obliged. It was painful to watch as she hit the ball again … and again … and again … and again. I think she must have hit the ball more than 20 times before she finally got it in the hole. Then, once done, we had to stay for a penalty period equal to how many times over par she had gone. Fifteen minutes later, we were finally free to go.

Now we knew we weren't anywhere near being first in the game, so we decided to take a detour to try to find one of the nearby Temptation caches. We were FTF. What a surprise!

With the coordinates to our next challenge in hand, we turned our car around and headed toward Chilliwack, our home. The coordinates led us to a familiar trail along the Vedder

River, where many locals enjoy their weekend walks and bike rides. When we arrived, we were given an option. We could walk to where the cache was place, or we could ride a bike. I looked at the distance to where the cache was placed. A kilometer away!?! I hopped on the bike, quickly made the find, and returned to my family ready to go on to our next stop.

We thought, surely, this must have been the last challenge. But we were wrong. Upon reaching our next stop, we discovered that we had to make a choice. Either one of us must swim (and dive) to get the next clue or we must use the one available kayak. But there was a lineup to use the kayaks at the lake. Erised, a strong swimmer, swam out to get the cache, and received the directions to our final destination.

Now, we made our way to the last leg of the race. We sped off in our car, and arrived at the final – a familiar site in Chilliwack, the Cultus Lake family park area. There, friends were gathering, enjoying a celebratory BBQ. There was food, drinks, and lots of friends, both new and old. And while Family Extremes weren't the first to finish (we came in seventh) the finish was fun!

# First, Best, Geo-buddy

Sarah Murphy
*sarahmur*


The first voice that a baby can hear,
is the dulcet tones of your mother dear.
The first kiss pressed on to your head,
is your mom's goodnight as you lay in bed.
The first warm hand that, with love, holds yours,
with a smile and a laugh is always hers.
The first big fight you'll have as a teen,
you'll yell at your mom, "That's not what I mean!"
The first advice you'll seek when you're grown,
is your mom's as you're crying into the phone.

For some lucky ones, your mom will be
your very first geocaching buddy.
She'll race out the door for First to Find
and shout 'found it' when you're losing your mind.
She'll go hiking for hours in the trees
And her famous phrase is 'One more cache, please!'
She gets it more than your other half
how fun caching is and how much of a laugh.

When you don't want to cache all on your own,
why not ask your mother to go along?
If you're lucky, like me, she might just be
your first, and your best, geo-buddy!

# Don't Fear the Ghost

Kimberly Eldredge
*TippySheep*

We'd been planning the trip for months. Research had been compiled, supplies had been purchased, permits secured, and cameras charged. It would be epic, it would be something new, it would be two days with just me and my dad...

It was probably April when Dad heard about the trip: kayaking the Colorado River from Hoover Dam to Willow Beach. It was a total trip of thirteen miles, three hot springs, two sets of rapids, and is the perfect place to see Rocky Mountain Sheep.

And it was my first encounter with a ghost.

This stretch of the Colorado River runs through a National Monument. In the preparation, we'd discussed placing a geocache to commemorate the trip but upon some more research discovered that National Monuments, being run by the National Park Service, didn't allow for the placement of any new geocaches. Since we're not only good stewards of Public Lands but also ran several prominent websites about outdoor recreation, we knew that geocaching just wouldn't be part of the adventure.

But there was a ghost.

Our first day of kayaking brought visits to hots springs, exploring an abandoned tunnel that dead ended in a thermal spring, being observed by Rocky Mountain Sheep, and being too busy to eat lunch. I'm NEVER too busy to eat.

As we found a small beach, just big enough for our tent, the clouds thickened. It had been overcast all day – the perfect weather to bring out the sheep and keep the day from getting too hot. Even in November, the Nevada/Arizona boarder is hot.

I was so hungry. I was nearly in tears when dad decided that we needed to set up the tent before getting out the brand new backpacking stove and the envelopes of freeze dried heaven that would be dinner. It was the first time setting up the tent and it seemed to take forever. Especially when the wind came up and we needed to stake out the rainfly and fill the tent with our gear to keep it from blowing into the river. Then we had to make sure the kayaks were completely tied up. Our outfitter warned us that the river could rise as much as TEN FEET in as little as an hour when the water flow from the Hoover Dam was adjusted – depending on the power needs from distant Las Vegas.

Finally! Finally dinner.

That little camp stove seemed to take forever to boil the water. The ten minutes of waiting for the hot water to rehydrate the freeze dried pre-packaged meal was torture.

The wind was picking up. Then a few drops started blowing in sideways. Cold rain in my ear and hot noodles on my tongue. By the time we were done with dinner, it was raining. By the time the dishes were put away and the kayaks unloaded it was POURING.

Dad and I huddled in a little gully under raid coats, sitting uncomfortably on three-legged camp stools. I could hear the water starting to rush from the hills above the canyon to start to trickle into the gully. First a trickle, then up to my shoes, over my ankles...

When the lightning hit the canyon wall on the other side of the river I dove into the dubious shelter of the tent, listening for the river to rise up and swallow us, tents, kayaks, and all.

And through my dreams, a ghost flickered in and out.

The next day dawned with that clarity that only a morning after a storm brings. Tea (with sand in it) never tasted so good. Freeze dried eggs… nothing makes those palatable.

Finally on the river again, mid-morning. Thankfully, Ringbolt Rapids had all but disappeared in the night, the river's flow calm, easy, and steady. With a dam up stream, even the extra water from the storm hadn't raised the water flow that much.

This would be the day with the ghost. My first ghost. Maybe the last ghost…

It is cache, "A Tale of Two Signs" (GC69E0), and the only cache anywhere along our route.

The description reads:

> *You've got to find this one by boat. The coordinates were taken from the middle of the Colorado River. There are two signs on either side of the river that can be read when your boat reaches these coordinates.*

No problem I thought! How hard can it be to paddle the river, watch the GPS, and snap a photo of a SIGN at just the right moment? It's a frickin' SIGN – not like it moves!

*Right?*

What I forgot was that I would be moving…

By the time I got the GPS and the camera (for proof we were there) out of the water-tight box it was almost too late. Powering it up and getting a signal seemed to take forever, all the while the current pushed us relentlessly onward, getting closer and closer to the ghost.

Maybe the GPS wasn't very accurate. Maybe the coordinates were off. But thankfully, my dad was able to shout out that he'd spotted the two signs. I was able to whip out my camera and stretch the minimal zoom opt the end of its capabilities to snap the photos. The proof. The sign.

And coming home, I was able to claim my first ghost.

# The Castaways

Kent Van Cleave
*psyprof*

On January 6, 2012, I (psyprof) met up with DMflyer to go after the Castaway series of geocaches on a cluster of islands in Cherokee Lake, just north of Morristown, Tennessee. DMflyer is from Gate City, Virginia, and I live just east of Knoxville, Tennessee. I arrived at the Cedar Hill Boat Dock late morning, my canoe on the back of my truck, and DMflyer was already there. I had not met DMflyer before, but knew him to be one of the most active cachers in Tennessee (presently with nearly 11,000 finds and 700 caches owned). I would be caching with geo-royalty.

It was a mild January day, temperature in the mid-fifties, with a light breeze across the lake from the southwest. We set out from the boat dock just off the southwest end of Panther Creek State Park. The shoreline is jagged, as the waterline contours the nearly-mountainous terrain. The boat dock sits on the side of a long cove, protruding into the shoreline along the bed of what was once a creek. Looking down this elongated slough, we could see the islands dead ahead, out on the open waters of the lake. In the cove, sheltered by land from the wind, the water was mostly calm, and the paddling was easy. I was pleased about this, because I needed to assess how comfortable and competent this stranger would be in a canoe.

Not far ahead, on the right, we arrived at GCV1KGBR - Crocodile Rock Cache, on the shoreline of Panther Creek State Park. That was our first stop. By now, I felt DMflyer would be a good crew member; now I would see how well we work together hunting for a cache. DMflyer had already found this cache nearly two years earlier, at a time when the water was low, but his prior find meant nothing, given the nature of the terrain we were searching - a jumble of jagged rock formations normally under water, but now exposed. It took us nearly an hour to find the cache.

> **Psyprof:** *I tried this cache in early summer, and the water was too high. Out today with DMflyer to get the castaway series, put the trusty canoe in at the boat dock, and got this first. DMflyer said the coords were way off, and we hunted all over the area. Was giving up and returning to canoe when I spotted it, not ten feet from where we beached. TFTC!*

There are six caches on the cluster of islands, in a roughly double line, going from northeast to southwest, following the natural terrain of the Appalachian region. The southernmost island is long and narrow. It runs a mile, northeast to southwest, with a much smaller island just northeast. Along that line lie four caches, one on the smallest island. A second island, larger in area, lies northwest of the first, separated by a passage a few hundred yards wide. On its southwest end, the island is half-way bisected by a long slough. Two caches are on that island. Poison ivy is plentiful on all of the islands so we were glad it was winter and it all died back.

As we set out again, we agreed that we would start northeast and work our way southwest, getting the cache on the smallest island first. We would then get the first two caches on the long island, cross the passage to the larger island and get the two caches there, before returning to the southwest end of the longer island for the last cache. Of the two caches we would find on the larger island, the first would require beaching along the passage between the islands, then walking across a wooded area to the end of the slough that cuts into the island. The second cache there lies at the southwest-most point of that island. For the last cache, we would round the end of the long island, and beach on the shoreline closest to the cache.

The cache on the small island is GC263ZM Castaway #4: All By Myself and is rated 1.5 difficulty, 5 terrain. After we cleared the shoreline onto the open lake, we turned almost due north, and the cache lay about a half mile ahead of us. There was a quartering breeze of four or five knots, hitting our left rear, and a light chop on the lake. The breeze helped propel us along to the small island. In the summer, boaters like to beach here to hang out.

We found this cache pretty quickly then set out for the next one.

> *Dmflyer: 13:53:00 First find on my birthday. Our Cherokee Canoe turned out great. Weather cooperated, sun came out and very little wind. Took a few minutes to find. Log was a little damp. We dried it out some.*

Back in the canoe, we rounded the northeast-most point of the long island, and proceeded into the passage between the islands. The second cache we would find there, GC263XT Castaway #1: Rock Hotel a 2 difficulty, 5 terrain, lay near the northeast end of the long island, up in the woods. It did not take long to find it.

> *psyprof: Found with DMflyer on a perfect day - and his birthday.*

> *Dmflyer: "Second find on my birthday... Went right to this one. Nice cache, been a while since it was found. (10/16/2010)"*

Then we headed for GC263YH Castaway #2: The Old Homestead another 2 difficulty, 5 terrain, half way down the long island and up in the woods off the beach. There were indeed traces of an old homestead there. I thought of the people who had set out to make a life here, and then were forced to move by the creation of the lake. It took us a while to find it, but find it we did.

> ***Dmflyer:*** *14:28 Saw the daffodils, and a few other things :)*

Next, we crossed the passage to the other large island. We beached the canoe in a cove, then crossed a wooded hill, emerging from the woods onto the beach at the terminus of the slough. As we searched for the first of this island's caches, GC26ZX7 Castway #6: In the Ivy another 2 difficulty, 5 terrain. I noticed a medium sized sailboat, a Boston Whaler large enough for a cabin, on the beach a couple hundred yards ahead. It appeared to be deserted as I walked up on it, but I hailed it loudly just in case someone was asleep inside. Getting no response, I turned and called out loudly in the direction of the woods. Still I received no response.

By now, a stiffer breeze had arisen, sweeping up the slough, so any call I made I knew would be swept away. I also noted that one could not see the opening of the slough from where the boat was beached, so people could easily motor past the end of the slough and never see the sailboat.

DMflyer and I conferred. I had good cell phone signal, so I had a friend look up the Hamblen County Sheriff's non-emergency phone number. The Sheriff's office referred me to Tennessee Wildlife Resource Agency, who are responsible for boats and boating. I called TWRA, explained the situation, and gave them my home phone number, the registration number of the boat, and coordinates from my GPS. Then we turned back into the woods and found the cache.

> ***psyprof:*** *Found on a run with DMFlyer. It was from this cache that we spotted a sailboat drifted up on the*

*beach. We called TWRA with the lat-long and the registration number...*

**Dmflyer:** *14:37 It was a perfect day for caching on the lake. Mild temperatures, not too much wind - when we started - and the poison ivy was all died back.*

A quarter mile farther down this island lay our next objective, GC26ZWR Castaway #5: For the Birds 1.5 difficulty, 5 terrain.. By now the breeze was coming more strongly, and the chop had become small waves. Because the lake level was low, we encountered very shallow water and broad expanses of mud. Seeking first to go after this cache from the beach on the slough, we were repelled by rocks and mud, so we opted to round the point into the slough on which we had found the sailboat. But we could not simply turn northwest and then north around the point, because that would put us broadside to the wind and the now substantial waves, and swamp us. So we were forced to tack.

We quartered into the wind until we were far out enough to be able to quickly come about and then run downwind to the site where we would beach. We found the cache pretty quickly, but with "complications":

**psyprof:** *...I was amazed by the number of spiders and stink bugs in the cache!*

**Dmflyer:** *15:02 Finally made it to the point. We had a great time playing in the mud on the way to this one. Found a sailboat adrift on the way. Cache hiding spot full of spiders and stinkbugs. After I got rid of a few spiders, we signed the log.*

Now we would round the southwest tip of the long island in order to claim the last cache on it, GC263Z5 Castaway #3: The Middle of Nowhere 2.5 difficulty and a 5 terrain. Again, we could not simply clear the point and turn southeast, which would put us broadside to the waves, so we had to go into the wind again, then tack back to clear the point of the island. This was an effective strategy, but with both of us paddling in the heavy waves, the canoe was too unstable.

I had to have DMflyer just sit still, while I did all the paddling. I snapped my paddle in two as I exerted; good thing I always carry a spare! Finally, after a long paddle to the southwest, we were able to come about and run downwind, and DMflyer was able to resume paddling. We beached, walked into the woods, and found the cache after several minutes.

> **psyprof:** *"...After we hunted for the cache for several minutes, I walked away from the cache and 'walked a tangent', a straight line intended to pass about 20 feet south of the cache. When the feet to cache reading reached its lowest point I made a 90 degree turn and walked right to it.*

> **Dmflyer:** *15:34 We looked way too long for this one. Had we come up from the beach in the right spot, we would have seen it right away. Glad we found it though.*

We celebrated finding the entire series with no DNFs, then headed for the landing. We had about two hours of daylight left, and once again could not go by the most direct route. With the wind still strong, and the waves high, we had to tack several times as we crossed to the cove, adding lots of distance to the paddle. We did finally enter the shelter of the cove, and, very tired, got the canoe onto my truck just at dusk.

I drove the hour back to my house, as DMflyer drove the hour and a half to his, reflecting on the fun we had today and wondering what would happen with the boat. Arriving home, exhausted and muddy, I found a message on my answering machine. It was the sailboat owner, thanking me for reuniting him with his errant Boston Whaler!

# My First "Canoe" Outing

Freddie Crusoe
*cruiser5*

It was my first canoe outing to find a geocache.
Perhaps I should call it a "non-canoe" outing. I was caching in
an area about 40 minutes from my hometown on a fine October
day when this cache popped up on my caching app. I noticed it
only had three finds and there had been a lot of time between
finds. It was named Canoe Outing. After reading the
description, and being a rather adventurous gal, I decided I
needed to look into this cache, canoe or no canoe. This should
have been my clue that it could be challenging.

The first part of the adventure began as I was looking for a
parking spot within walking distance. I found a spot in a public
hunting ground and let my GPS do the trick to get me closer to
the cache. It was a lovely 70 degree day, so my t-shirt and jeans
were perfect for this adventure. Walking through the woods I
felt the calm that always came over me; I become one with
nature and enjoy every little thing around me. Little did I know
how much I would become one with nature!

I love caching with friends; yet solo caching holds a special
place in my heart. On this day I must say it was probably a

good thing as I was about to have one of the craziest experiences I have had geocaching up to date. The opening line for this cache (GC3RFRX) reads:

*Looking for an adventure? Then grab a canoe or kayak and hit the river! This beautiful stretch of river is a perfect getaway to relax and enjoy nature at its finest.*

Let's just say, it didn't let me down!

I didn't have a canoe or a kayak, but I grew up spending lots of time in a river. Since I was so close I just had to go for it; I hated to leave any caches behind. Once I made my way across the hunting land, I was surprised to find a huge fence blocking my path. Since I am short in stature and the fence carried a row of barbed wire across the top, I knew I wouldn't be climbing it.

Not to be thwarted, I turned to the left and followed the fence line to the river, thinking I could slip around the end of the fence and walk the river bank. Well when I got to the river bank imagine my surprise when the fence went directly down into the river. I walked a few hundred feet more and found a place I could cross. Tucking my GPS safely away on the upper part of my body, I stripped off my shoes, socks, and jeans and bundled them up before crossing the river. The water was a little chilly and as murky as any other river I had seen. Once I hit the center point of the river I was feeling pretty elated, then one more step and whoops! Up and over my hips! Brrrr!

Well now I was wet! No sense in turning back so I crossed over to the sandy shore on the other side. The sun was warm and it would dry my underwear fairly quickly. I was really thankful it wasn't hunting season, since I was now parading down the shoreline in wet underwear. Following my GPS a few hundred feet more, I discovered I was going to have to cross the river one more time. This time I found a much shallower point to cross where I could see the bottom all the way across. No surprises here! The cows in the nearby pasture where calling out a welcome or maybe they were laughing at me!

Once across the river, I noticed I was going to have to crawl under a fence and walk through a pasture. I sat on the grassy bank and put my shoes on and then proceeded to cross the pasture. I noticed several piles of dung, but wasn't sure what type of animal was leaving it. Looking around to be sure no animal was going to surprise me, I quickly crossed the pasture, avoiding the dung piles. Thankfully I didn't encounter any strange animals!

Looking at my GPS, I was pleased when noticed I was within a couple hundred feet of the cache. As I neared its location I sighed in exasperation. What? I had to cross the river again!

It was then that I noticed a strange sound! What was it? Not something I had ever heard before, my mind jumped to the thought of a wild boar? Wild, in a pasture? Or maybe it was in the pasture across the river where the cache was? Would somebody really be raising wild boars? I was so close now; I didn't want to leave without the cache.

I hurriedly slid under the fence and dropped my clothes bundle on the sand bar next to the river's edge. Stripping off my shoes, I waded in to cross the river. I kept hearing the noise over and over, although I still wasn't able to decipher what it was. Making it to ground zero and hurriedly retrieved the cache, I was excited to find a pathtag inside. I dropped in a piece of swag and signed the log, all the while looking over my shoulder for whatever wild animal was making the horrible noise! Happy to have my smiley I couldn't wait to get back across the river and out of there!

The return trip crossing the pasture, doing the limbo under the fence,s and crossing the river two more times were uneventful. For the sixth and final trek across the river, I decided not to cross at my original point since I was still trying to let the sun and breeze dry my underwear. I walked a bit further down the bank and noticed a nice shallow sandy spot to cross over. Success!

Wait! Are you kidding me? I waded across the river right into a very steep bank. When I had looked for a shallow place to cross, it never dawned on me to look at the other side of the river to see what the terrain was! Now my only option was up! Grabbing vines, tree roots, and long hunks of grass, I managed to scramble my way up the steep bank in my bare feet. Then I carefully picked my way over to my original crossing point.

This spot was once used as a party place and the remnants remained. I found a partially exposed tire and stood on that to scrub my now dirty feet and slip on my socks and shoes.

Now I was prepared to make the final trek to my car. I must have looked like quite the sight crossing the woods in my socks and underwear! Walking through the trees, it finally dawned on me what the noise was that lead my mind to jump to conclusions of wild boars living nearby. Two branches high overhead were grinding together! Laughing at myself, I just shook my head and smiled.

When I was about two hundred feet from the car, I realized my underwear remained pretty wet. I knew it would be uncomfortable under my jeans, so standing behind a huge upturned tree root, I stripped them off donned my jeans and walked to my car. I hopped inside and headed off down the road, smiling at my accomplishment and adventure all rolled into one! I couldn't wait to share this story with my geo-friends!

# Three Hour Tour

LA Newell
*J&LA*

The state's longest unfound cache had been sitting
there for exactly 2 years the day we stumbled across the listing:
Gilligan's Island (GC4X1K9). It was located in the romantic
town of Valentine, Nebraska, about 5 hours away. Not only had
it been lonely all this time, having remained solitary for so
long, but it was also my favorite kind: a puzzle cache.

Surprisingly enough, I recognized some key pieces of info
on the page. Shortly thereafter, I was holding the coordinates in
my hand, wondering about a possible springtime retrieval. I
contacted the CO who confirmed it would require a trek
through hip- to waist-high water, but unfortunately, it was mid-
January when our temps average colder than Alaska, when hell
freezes over & boogers turn to snotcicles. No one – including
the owner - had any expectation that it'd be attempted before
the seasonal warm up. This particular week, it'd barely escaped
freezing; there was snow on the ground, and I was bundled up
in boots and a heavy parka. Not exactly swimming or kayaking
weather.

A few days later, we were planning a trip to the panhandle

with "Jimmy63" to sign The 2.0 D & T Challenge (GC33YAZ), so we figured we'd at least take a quick peek at this cache on the way out. Jimmy, however, had another plan.

We picked him up along the way in O'Neill, and learned he'd brought everything we could possibly need to go after the cache , including water shoes, a towel and swim trunks. (Really?!) He wanted to get it for all of us, and we didn't even have to offer him a Coconut Cream Pie!

We arrived at the trailhead, and the air was whistling pretty hard from the North. The wind-chill was definitely a factor, and the cloud cover was fairly heavy - typical winter weather. The trail was high above everything around it; you could see for several miles. The view was spectacular with the white snow, yellow prairie grasses and black evergreens all around.

As we approached the Niobrara River, we decided to stay on the trail to spy the uncharted isle from atop a colossal, turn-of-the-century railroad bridge ahead. It was amazing in its rusted glory, looming above everything else around it. The river valley below looked treacherous, but maybe passable. It was worth a shot.

Jimmy answered the call of nature from the magnificent bridge before we headed back to the trail. Of course, I thought it was hilarious and, much to his chagrin, I absolutely had to include that little detail whenever I retold this story. . It wasn't my fault he didn't remember he'd have to swim through that particular stream later! (LOL)

At the abutment, we had the choice of backtracking to a safer route or attempting an uncontrolled slip-n-slide down the slick, muddy incline. All voted for the more dangerous option.

So down we went on our behinds, tossing boots and gear along as we went. We hiked around the towering bridge supports, through knee-deep snow, over barbed wire, around obstacles, through gates, past a handful of historical sites, and down the embankment to the water's edge. The current was zipping along swiftly.

MaryAnn (I) took a position upstream, poised with the cell phone on 9-1-1 speed dial and holding the camera, while the Skipper ("J") took watch downstream, prepared to take action in case of a water-rescue scenario. Gilligan ("Jimmy63") got ready, tossing his dry clothes haphazardly into the snow and his cell phone into a dry box.

The water was bitter cold and slightly shallower than expected. Jim stepped in with a puff of discomfort, and then gingerly worked his way across the river asking aloud, "What was I thinking this time of year?" Just before reaching the island, he plummeted unexpectedly into the water, appearing to be stuck on something and getting pushed over by the current. We were both ready to spring into action when he managed to free himself and clamber onto the island. Come to find out later, he'd been sucked into quicksand along the river's floor - possibly due to the natural springs in the area. He would've lost his shoe had it not been tied tightly. We knew it could've been much worse though. There was every possibility he could've gotten inundated and found himself in hypothermic shock, or drowned. Luckily, both he and his smartphone escaped unscathed.

He found the cache in good shape, and grabbed the baggie full of toys as his prize. "I took it all!" he proclaimed. After a few moments of psyching himself up, he hopped into the water again, this time shuffling hastily across the quicksand. He was cussing like a sailor (pun intended) while J bleeped him out for the video I was filming. Just off shore, before getting out, Jimmy threatened to splash us to show how "nice" the water was. He climbed ashore, grabbed his towel and ended our adventure with, "I can't feel my legs. I feel something ... I, I think they're legs. Now I'm gonna get naked and into some warm, dry clothes."

I ended the video there.

This was our first epic FTF, and the cache's first 2 favorite points.

# Down the River with Just One Paddle

Gerhard Wetzel
*gw0143*

Dr. Moro and I were having a great time. It was a sunny mid-August evening in New Hampshire, and we were about to head down the Merrimack River in my inflatable double kayak. Earlier in the day, we had scored our very first FTF in New Hampshire and gone on to find 20 more caches. Life was good!

It was already 5 pm when we got to the boat launch area near the Fisher Cats stadium in Manchester, NH. We took a look at the river, which was perfectly calm, then looked at the bulky life vests we had brought along. Deciding they would just make us too hot and sure that we wouldn't need them, we left them behind.

Our targets on the river were five caches in the "MRCC" (Merrimack River Canoe Caches) series, #2-#6, a total of about eight miles of paddling, which was plenty for us, especially in an inflatable. Plus, there was virtually no current, so the going was slow. We were a little concerned about time, but it was supposed to stay light until at least 8:30 pm and we figured we'd be able to go eight miles in 2 1/2 hours. That would also leave another hour for finding the caches.

We found MRCC #2 (GC1J239) through #5 (GC1J25Z) without incident. They were all on scenic little islands in the river, whose water level was fairly low, making the islands larger than usual, with lots of exposed rocks that looked pretty with the water flowing between them and some trees growing on the more permanent parts of the islands. The river banks in many places were steep, revealing eroded tree roots.

After finding MRCC #5, we noticed there were rapids ahead. For the most part the river had been very calm, and we had already made it through some minor currents without issue. But what lay ahead of us looked a bit more serious. Should we paddle over to shore, take out and walk around the rapids? Would that even be possible given the steep river banks? We were tired, we didn't have all that much daylight left, and clearly not much sense either, so we decided to just go for it. We re-launched the kayak from the island and quickly hit the first set of rapids.

Whee! "Oh, that was fun," I thought, a little wet from the water splashing into the boat.

"It's not over yet!" Dr. Moro exclaimed. He was sitting up front and had a much better view of the large, partially submerged rock our kayak was about to hit.

One nice thing about inflatables is that they can be very stable. At least in calm waters. On a lake, or even a river without a current, you pretty much can't fall in, unless you deliberately jump overboard. Inflatables are also not a bad choice for going over submerged rocks - the water generally rubs the rocks fairly smooth, so punctures are not usually a concern. I had never fallen in while kayaking in an inflatable before.

Well, there is a first time for everything!

As the inflatable hit the rock ahead of us, it did what inflatables do best – it remained flexible and adjusted to the obstacle. In this case, that meant wrapping around the rock. The problem with that was that the front of the kayak was effectively stuck on the rock, but the rear was still being pushed by the strong current of the rapids.

Dr. Moro was ejected from his seat first. I quickly followed.

Being dumped into rapids is not a pleasant experience - water swirling around and above your head, submerged rocks close to the surface hitting and scraping your knees. But I managed to stay afloat without too much trouble - in spite of the now clearly imprudent decision not to wear a life vest. I let the current carry me to calmer waters.

But then I looked over to Dr. Moro, and to my surprise, he was struggling. He is a much better swimmer than I am, but somehow the current was dragging him under rather than just along, as it had me. He was clearly in distress, his head disappearing under water and then bobbing up again several times. There was nothing I could do - I was too far away, and there was no way I would be able to fight the current.

Finally, the strong current released Dr. Moro, and he was able to catch his breath. He waved, signaling that he was OK and swam over to solid ground to rest.

It suddenly dawned on me that we had gone into the rapids entirely unprepared and that all our belongings had been loose. I checked the pockets of my swim trunks - my Delorme PN-60 was still there. It was supposedly waterproof, but I wasn't sure just how waterproof. To my amazement, it was still on underwater, and it showed my current position in the river. My camera was in my other pocket. It, too, was waterproof, and I had used it before to take underwater pictures, so I was mainly concerned with it not falling out of my pocket.

I eventually managed to get a foothold somewhere on a rock and saw the flipped over kayak headed my way. I grabbed it, turned it over and climbed in. A ziplock baggie was floating next to the kayak. I was thrilled to find that it contained our car keys, placed there by Dr. Moro back at the launch. We had not, however, secured the baggie to the boat so we were lucky it had stayed close to it - and also that there was evidently enough air inside to make it float!

I needed paddles. I noticed the bright red one that Dr. Moro had been using floating downstream of my position. No sign of the black paddle I had been using anywhere. I tried to use my hands to make the kayak catch up with the paddle, but to no avail. So I decided to get back into the river and swim to the paddle. Fortunately, I was able to catch up with it, albeit slowly. Meanwhile, the kayak had gotten stuck on a tree upstream, so I then had to swim back with the paddle to the boat. I only noticed then that the paddle had Dr. Moro's towel wrapped around it - another item we could have easily lost to the river.

I got back in the boat and paddled to where Dr. Moro was on shore, still resting and a bit shaken from his near-drowning. He was also taking inventory of his losses - his camera was on him, but had gotten wet and unfortunately was not waterproof. At least he would still be able to retrieve the photos he had taken thus far from the memory card. He had also lost the only pen we had with us to sign the cache logs.

We searched for the second paddle along both shorelines for a little while, but eventually gave up on it. With just one paddle, our progress down the river was much slower. We had already lost a lot of time in the flip-over incident and its aftermath, and now the sun was setting and it was starting to get dark.

Despite everything we'd been through, and the impending darkness, did we still want to go after MRCC #6 (GC1J26H)? Of course we did! Otherwise we would have (almost) drowned in vain - and we might have to come back and navigate those rapids again, something we definitely didn't want to do. But when we made it to "GZ", it was too dark to see anything. I decided to take flash pictures with my camera and then see if they showed anything interesting. One did! There it was; we had found the cache that had caused us all this grief! We took a picture of the log since we didn't have a pen anymore, and Dr. Moro left his signature item, a 5-yen good-luck coin for the next intrepid (or foolish?) visitor.

Back on the river, it was very slow going with just one paddle, and we still had more than two miles ahead of us. We started worrying about additional rapids. It would be virtually impossible to see them in the dark, and every sound of water rushing scared us. We sure didn't want to flip over again! So we considered bailing out. But where? And that's when we spotted some lights on shore - a family fishing.

We approached them and asked if it was possible to exit the river there. They said it probably was, so we got out and dragged the kayak up the somewhat steep river bank to the street. We ended up calling a taxi to take us back to my car, then picked up Dr. Moro's car on the way back and finally arrived back home around midnight.

Our first flipping over experience while kayaking, and, in Dr. Moro's words from his log, "our most unforgettable Geo-adventure, ever."

# Kayak Trek 2015

Jennelle Black
*Netnet*

**My tale starts in the state of Michigan.** My older brother, the one who got me started in geocaching and head of this event, Addham, invited me to his home turf to kayak the Pere Marquette River in Baldwin, Michigan. Being from Illinois, I was in for a fantastic outdoor treat.

I had been to a few geocaching events before, mostly lunch stops and one great three part series called The Evil Cachernapper. But none of my caching experiences compared to Kayak Trek 2015. This would be my first over-night cache event and the second annual kayak trek hosted by a group of very avid cachers. I knew, with my measly 100 caches and the group with the average of 5,000, I would learn some important caching tips.

We made our way to laker91's abode, filling up the trailer with four kayaks and plenty of gear. Our group consisted of mikeymac0908, laker91, gregg1199, Addham, Krazy_Kidz, fastpitschfamily, and jomber. Along with another car and three more kayaks, we made the hour drive and a stop for lunch. In all the excitement, we were at the loading dock ready to get in the water in no time.

The first day was a beautiful and sunny 80 degrees. Although it was late August, the water was decently warm. Having never stepped foot in a kayak before, I was doing remarkably well. Everyone kept saying to me, "You will no doubt tip your kayak on your first time out" but I was determined not to let that happen.

Mikeymac0908 eventually did tip, but he wasn't the only one to get wet; there was one stop on the river was deep enough to swim. We all took a break and pushed our kayaks on a sandy beach. There was a tall cliff so a few from our group raced to the top. Some of us enjoyed adult beverages along the trail, which made for very interesting comments.

I heard grown men singing "Just around the river bend" from the movie 'Pocahontas' more than anyone ever should.

The first leg of the trip was a long nine miles and we got seven caches. We made our stop for the night at Gleason's Landing, where Krazy_Kidz's family had a well-deserved fire ready to go for us to make our dinners. We set up our tents, ate, and sat around the fire playing cards and talking until, one by one, we headed to bed. It was a little chilly that night but I curled up in my sleeping bag and drifted off to sleep. Little did we know, the first day would be the better of the two.

The second morning was an early, chilly start. A few of our crew woke up to discover raccoons had made off with ramen noodles, Twizzlers, and trail mix. We cleaned up the best we could, packed up the tents and bags, and we were off.

Not long down the river, the clouds got dark. The beautiful 80 degrees from the day before turned into a gloomy 65. Then it started to sprinkle, then to rain, then to pour

We persevered, thinking the skies would open up any moment to pure blue. (Which didn't happen for hours!)

That second day consisted of fourteen miles, nine caches, a few small rapids, one big thunderstorm, and way overusing the phrase, "Are we there yet?" not to mention a steady chant of "How many more miles left?"

At one point, we even had to make a pit stop at Rainbow Rapids camping site for the thunder and lightning to subside.

We made the steep climb up the road to a latrine and another cache, had a quick bite to eat, and decided the rain wouldn't actually stop. So we hit the river again!

If we weren't already soaked, both Krazy_Kidz and Addham tipped their kayaks this day.

The blue skies finally appeared after our final stop for the day, Upper Branch Bridge. Some changed into dry clothes, some of us, unfortunately, didn't pack any extra. I was one of the ones who did.

Some of the things I learned from that fateful trip:

Don't rely on your phone to keep the battery life for the trip.

Bring a real life camera if you want pictures.

Pack easy food that doesn't need to be refrigerated or cooked!

Make sure you check the weather reports.

Sure you can tough through cold temperatures and soaked clothing, but nothing beats a nice dry extra set of clothes and a warm sweatshirt for the middle of the night!

Plans are already in motion for the third annual Geocaching Kayak Trek and even though my previous experience was so wet, I'm excited to join the crew again.

# First Geocaching S.O.S. Call

Laura Ready
*Wa wa*

We've all done it: you're so focused on getting to a cache, you lose track of all potential dangers. Before you know it, you're suddenly wondering not only how you got there in the first place, but how you're ever going to get back out!

This is the story of my first caching S.O.S call, having put myself in serious danger.

When you take a fair skinned Irish Geocacher on a DT grid-filling mission who is used to the mild climate of rainy Dublin, Ireland, and plonk her in the middle of the island of sunny Malta, there is already potential for trouble. Especially one who is on her own mission to complete her D/T grid.

I had a cache on my radar called "All The Jokes" GC1JMNP. I really wanted to find it, as it ticked a box for me. but access on foot was proving a little bit problematic. The previous day, I had tried a different approach to get to cache from the from the cliffs above my head, not realizing that an impossible descent was required.

I was up on a hilltop in the afternoon sun in Mellelia, enjoying the spectacular views along the coastline on a rocky trail. I spotted another trial that seemed to lead directly to the "All the Jokers" cache. It was over a kilometer away. A kilometer is nothing to walk in the milder climate of Ireland, but it is a different kettle of fish in extreme heat.

I decided to go for it.

I headed off, totally underestimating how much water I would need. I hadn't really prepared properly; I had no Garmin and my phone was only half charged. The battery pack was in the hotel. But I did have two full bottles of water, and assumed I'd be grand… as you do.

I took my time along the uneven path. I climbed down a hill and back up another, and found a new trail. The sky was cloudless and blue, the sun was beating down on my back and the sea was the most lovely shade of cerulean blue. The views of the coastline to be seen en route were simply spectacular from my narrow rocky half road, half trail that wound along the cliff face.

The peacefulness soon came to an abrupt end.

There was a dog under a van where the trail ended. He didn't look happy to see me and he barked his head off. I was frightened. I was only 245 meters or so away from the cache, so I left the path to swing around higher than the dog when another one came barking. I was suddenly cornered by the pair of them.

I called out to see if the owner was nearby, talked nicely to the dogs and simultaneously grabbed a stick for defense. Thankfully, a head popped up from a field nearby and called to the dogs. I skedaddled while the coast was clear, but was then firmly off the trail and in the wilderness.

I had to climb through some trees, balance along a water storage wall, and go over a wall or two in my attempt to get back to the track. I ended up on a cliff edge overlooking a gorge 83 meters away from GZ. It looked too dangerous to attempt without equipment (preferably wings). This was the second time I gotten to within a 100m of the cache. Disappointed and tired, I turned back. It was only when I was trying to avoid the dogs that I spotted another potential roundabout way in.

I made the descent and the terrain totally changed. Now, I

had never even seen a surface or landscape like this one. I felt as if I had landed on another planet, possibly the moon. All around me was a smooth golden yellow limestone shelf with undulating humps and lumps with the biggest boulders I had ever seen dotted all around it. I walked along the stunning surface.

I was pretty tired by the time I got to GZ, and I felt a bit dizzy. I knew exactly what I needed to do: climb up on top of the biggest bolder to get the cache. Searching for a way, I also worried because my phone only had 10% battery and I was exhausted. Could I walk all the way back to the hotel?

I phoned the hubby to say where I was and to explain about the dying phone. While doing so, I noticed my remaining water bottle topple and empty before I could get to it. That's when I started to really panic. To get to the top of the boulder involved a leap – physically and of faith. I was too nervous and dizzy to complete the last 4 meters as my legs had turned to jelly - jumping was out of the question as the heat was taking its toll.

In fact, a wave of nausea and dizziness washed over me then and I began to feel very unwell. It was my first attack of heatstroke: it came suddenly and intensely, leaving me very weak. I got back on the dying phone to tell my husband I was in trouble, as I thought I was going to faint.

I abandoned the search for the cache despite being a few meters away. I felt very overheated. Slowly and with tired feet I made went back along limestone shelf and climbed back up the narrow trail to the road where I had first seen the farmer to see if I could get some water. He kindly let me refill my two water bottles from his spring. I downed one full bottle of lovely cool water right then and there, and filled it again. It helped, but I still felt unwell.

I started to walk back along the narrow path but waves of dizziness continued to wash over me, my legs were like jelly and I found myself swaying while walking. I didn't feel capable of walking all the way back. In fact all I wanted to do was just lie on the road and go asleep. With the last drain of the battery on my phone I called my husband. I told him where I was and where I was headed and asked him to get a taxi and meet me at the nearest landmark I could remember, which was a water treatment plant. The phone died mid-conversation and I hoped against hope that he had enough information to find me.

By the time I to the water treatment plant there, I could barely walk. I sat outside the plant slumped up against a wall. A kind man saw my distress and came out, inviting me inside to cool down and so I could use his phone. He sat with me, a real modern day knight!

The hubby finally arrived breathless, having more or less run from the hotel. He gave me a right lecture about geocaching mid-day sun madness. The people in Malta in the plant were so nice, even giving us a lift back to the hotel where I had a cool shower and a good cry, after the self-inflicted fright I experienced.

That being said, I was determined not to give up, having come so close. I hired a car and filled it with gallons of water. I took the hubby with me. We left early morning, while it was cooler. The half-road, half-track was terrifying to drive down, as the car seemed wider than it in places and there was a huge drop and no barrier. I was hyperventilating by the time we got to the end of the narrow track.

The dogs charged once more, but I knew their bark was worse than their bite. The same friendly farmer who called me a "mad" woman while letting me fill my water bottles rolled his eyes and waved. I didn't even need the Garmin. I knew exactly where to go.

The hubby was transfixed by the lunar landscape and stopped several times to give me geological updates and poke at stuff in the limestone. Then, he was up the rock face and triumphantly holding the cache before I could say "careful now"! Then, he laughed at my attempts.

I think this was one of my most captivating caches for or a number of reasons. I often wonder what it is about the caches that involve danger - or those we really struggle with - that make us like them so much. This one was a real physical challenge due to the heat and terrain, but an outstanding choice for a cache for geological reasons. It's as close as I will ever get to being on a lunar landscape. I also learned a few lessons about preparing better and always have a backup GPS now and spare batteries. I was glad I didn't collapse on that narrow track, knowing how close I had come to doing so.

After I logged my DNF and subsequent find, I got a lovely email from the CO saying how he really enjoyed reading my account of finding his cache. He said he would treasure my log forever.

There are some caches that need far more written about them than TFTC.

# Hey, Boo Boo!

Dan DeKoning
*DGDK*

**It was early morning,** Fourth of July, 2009. I had been working all weekend on gathering geocaches to cover the counties that I needed for the "Find a Geocache in Every County of Wisconsin Challenge," as well as for the DeLorme pages for the Wisconsin DeLorme Challenge.

The geocache on page 104 of the DeLorme Atlas brought me deep into the woods of the northern edge of Wisconsin. I had two options before searching it out: either suck it up and go for it, or give up on the challenge. I was already as far away from home as I could be and still be in the same state, so I wasn't going to give up.

Although it was July, because of the northern latitude, the temperature was cool. The mosquitoes and other bugs hadn't yet begun their day, and the woods were silent as I made my way to the geocache. It was a typical hide in the woods: not a trail to be found, other than that deer-made. I trudged through the underbrush, climbed over logs. At one point, a deep ravine separated me from the geocache, but that wasn't enough to hold back my desire to check off another DeLorme page.

Eventually I made it to ground zero. I sat down on a tree stump, took a bottle of water from my pack and had a drink while I rested. I was within thirty feet, now! I decided to cheat, and looked at the hint: "In a tree stump" was the long and short of it. This excited me even more, because I realized I was probably sitting right on top of it!

I wasn't.

It was then that I noticed that I was surrounded by tree stumps. There seemed to be a million of them, but in reality there were probably only fifty or so. I searched. I searched more. After what seemed to be hours, I finally shouted out a hearty "eureka" (to no one) and held aloft the most beautiful matchstick holder I had ever seen. I signed the log and stowed it back in its hidey hole.

It wasn't until after I found the cache that I noticed where I was. To the east of me was a sheer drop of a hundred feet into the Superior Falls section of the Montreal River. Beyond that, the state of Michigan. To the north was nothing but pine trees until they gave way to the shores of Lake Superior. The south and southeast were nothing but muck and marsh. That only left one way back to the car: following the ridge of the terrain through the pine to the southwest.

I followed the terrain back toward my car, back-tracking almost exactly the route that I had used to come in. As usual, when I hike the woods, I was watching the forest floor as I walked, to avoid getting tripped up by a big rock or an exposed root.

That's how I noticed it.

A pile of fresh, just-hit-the-ground scat. I had wandered around in the woods enough to know that it hadn't come from a deer, or anything smaller than one. I knew that there were only two possible sources of the scat: bear, or me. I was fairly certain I hadn't left it on the way in.

I stopped, stood in place, and scanned the woods around me for any movement. Listening, I could hear only the whisper of the wind moving through the pines. After a few minutes, I decided I was safe enough, and continued my journey.

I walked another hundred yards and entered a small clearing

in the woods. The blue sky opened above me, and the forest floor was awash in green. Then I noticed the bear.

It was standing directly in front of me. Had I seen it in a zoo, I would've thought nothing of seeing it. Just a common black bear, right? But out in the woods with no cell service, no protection to speak of, and no road or help to be found for another half mile, it was a completely different story.

The bear was easily six foot from tail to nose, weighing in at probably three hundred pounds. There I was, eye-to-eye with Ursa Make-Me-Pee-My-Pants ...

Time slowed to a stop as the bear stared directly at me, but my brain began moving at supersonic speed. Although my feet were planted firmly on the ground, in my mind's eye, I could see myself sprinting through the woods, fast enough to leave an after image just like you'd see in the cartoons.

But the logical part of my brain knew that running was NOT a good idea. I knew the bear could run me down like a ten year old kid running after the ice cream truck, cash in hand. I also knew that climbing a tree wasn't a viable option. I didn't know what to do.

My brain searched for ideas. I tried to remember what I had learned in the Boy Scouts about dealing with bears, and after a few seconds of panic, I remembered that I had never been in Boy Scouts.

I looked at the bear. The bear looked at me. I glared at the bear. The bear glared back. I smiled at the bear. The bear winked at me, and I was sure he was telling me we'd become best of friends.

Finally, I remembered something from a documentary I saw once. I put my hat on top of my walking stick, raised it and my other arm in the air and started waving them madly. Then I yelled at the top of my lungs, in my best Yogi Bear voice, "Hey Boo Boo, let's go find us a pic-a-nic basket!"

The bear stood there. It released a little huff out of its nose, and after a few seconds, turned and wandered into the woods.

That was the first time I had an up close and personal encounter with a bear on his own turf, and I hope that it's the last.

# My First Bear Encounter (Sort of)

Jason Meggs
*JakeAsh*

A few years ago, I was hiking through Pisgah National Forest in North Carolina. I was caching on an unfamiliar trail, which of course, is the best kind. It was very late Fall, some would say early Winter, at the time. The air was thin and chilly but perfectly clear. The views were amazing with the remaining red, orange, and yellow treetops in the distance. It was an awesome morning for hiking and caching.

I had a list of six, maybe seven geocaches saved in my phone for this particular adventure. Most of them were close to the trail according to my offline map. There was one, however, that was very much off the beaten path. It was number two on my way and I had not made up my mind about going for it when I reached the point where it looked like I should leave the trail, if I was going to do it. I stood and pondered. I knew I had limited time for the day, and it was going to be hard enough getting to all the caches along the trail in the time I had allotted myself. According to the cache description, there would be a lengthy bushwhack and a creek crossing, followed by stone formations I'd need to make my way around in order to find some small cave. It was going to be time consuming, but I decided it sounded too good to pass up. I typed the coordinates into my GPS and left the trail.

The brush was already thinned, being so late in the year, but the thorns were still in full brutality mode. I used my walking stick to make a temporary path as I made my way. I could hear the water babbling ahead in the creek. Progress. With only a minor scratch on the knuckle, I finally came to the water's edge. I had to stick a few fingers in to feel the temperature. Yep. It was as cold as it looked.

I planned each step across beforehand. I knew I had a long hike after this and did not want wet boots the rest of the way. Using my stick as a crutch to help balance, I made my way across to the large boulders on the other side. The stones varied in size from maybe 5 feet to 8 feet high, forming a wall of obstacles. I made my way through the rock maze and came to a thinly-wooded incline. I could tell on my GPS that I was closing in: only 65 more feet to the prize. With each step up the slight hill, I could see more of the rocky formation ahead. After a dozen steps or so, I could make out the top of a cave opening in the distance. Excellent. With each step higher, my view came further down the front opening.

When I reached about 20 feet away, near the bottom of the cave opening I saw dark ears, then brown eyes, and then a black nose. I froze in my tracks. It was the face of a black bear staring straight at me. "Ohhh crap," I whispered rather loudly. I saw no movement at all in the 3 seconds our eyes locked. I figured it was possibly waiting to see what I would do as well. I very slowly turned and quietly took a few steps down the hill looking at the stone wall I would have to quickly navigate through if that big guy gave chase. "But what if it's not a guy?" I thought. "What if it's a momma with a young one?" I'd heard how protective they can be, and I knew it could get really ugly, fast. She could come out of their shelter any second, and all I had was a walking stick. Could I defend myself from an attacking momma bear with a 5 foot stick? Of course, all those thoughts occurred in the split moment when the adrenaline first started pumping.

By the time I had quickly made my way back down to the creek side boulders, I had calmed myself, possibly too much. Because at that point, I started questioning what I had even seen: "Now I've come all this way. I know there is a cache right up that hill in or next to that shallow cave. Do I know for sure that was indeed a bear? I have to know for sure. I have to get another look," I reasoned. I slowly crept up the incline one soft step at a time. I made it to my previous elevation and looked hard. "Those look like bear ears above bear eyes over a bear snout. That's definitely fur on the top of that head. Am I insane? What am I doing?" I cautiously took one step closer. No response. I then took another. At that point, I could see the entire floor of the shallow cave only inches below that snout. "Is she laying in a hole?" One more step closer and I had to smile.

It was no bear at all. It was rocks, moss, and shadows all amazingly aligned to form an all-too-real image of a bear's head - only recognizable from that exact angle and elevation I had first viewed the beast.

I continued up to the rock formation with a huge grin on my face and searched the area only briefly before I found the Tupperware container I came for. SL. TNLN. I continued the trail and found all the caches on my list that morning.

It was an excellent caching day, and I will always remember the rush of my first experience coming face-to-"face" with a momma black bear.

# My First *(and hopefully last)* Run-in with Cows!

Sarah Leonard
*snoopyisboss*

It was just a normal Saturday. I was going out geocaching.

About thirty to forty miles away from home there were three circular cache series. There was a bonus cache for each series; you needed to collect information from some of the caches to work out the co-ordinates for the bonus. The bonuses from the three series then gave you more information to find a 'super bonus'. I had done two of the series and this Saturday was the day to do the final series and get that super bonus. It was promising to be quite an exciting day.

The caches were loaded onto the GPS using a pocket query, the car was packed - lunch, walking boots, trekking pole etc., plus the dog, and off I went.

I parked at the recommended parking and the dog and I set off on a lovely walk with some interesting and different cache containers and some varied hides. There was one cache that I didn't find because an electric fence had been erected and I wasn't prepared to negotiate that on my own. Because of this, I had one number missing for the bonus. But I thought I still had a good chance of finding it.

The field note that I'd entered onto my GPS for what turned out to be my last find of the day, of the series, and of the year, simply said 'COWS'.

I walked through a field on a public footpath. The dog was on the lead and close by when suddenly I saw cows running toward me. The next minute, they had knocked me to the ground, trampled on me, and left me battered and bruised with life-threatening injuries. Despite having broken both arms, I managed to get my phone out of my coat pocket and attempted to dial 999 for emergency. I had lost my glasses and I struggled to see the phone, let alone the numbers.

I had a few attempts at dialing and eventually decided that I couldn't get through, so I started to shout for help. The next minute, the operator was on the phone asking what I wanted help with. I told her I'd fallen over and couldn't get up. I must have gradually realized what had really happened.

My confused message to the operator made her think that I was making a hoax call but she soon realized that I was serious – I really had been trampled by cows!

I couldn't remember exactly where I was so she spent some time talking me through my journey that morning. Eventually, with the help and knowledge of the local police, they worked out where I was and after fifty minutes on the phone, I was rescued. I was taken to the hospital where my collapsed lung was treated and I had several operations to fix my broken jaw and other broken bones. I was then put on a ventilator on the intensive care unit where I stayed for two and a half weeks.

I presume the dog ran off and went into hiding when the cows attacked. She was missing for twenty-four hours and was found by my family and the police the following day. I didn't see my faithful caching partner again until nearly three weeks later, when my friends who were looking after her, came to visit me in the hospital and brought her with them.

I am very grateful that I don't remember those first few days; I was sedated and didn't 'wake up' until four days later.

News of my plight spread through various caching communities. Cards and messages started to flood in and soon there was nowhere to put them all. I received nearly one hundred cards and many of these were from geocachers. Some came from geocachers I didn't know and even from cachers abroad.

Once I was moved out of intensive care, I was able to have visitors other than family. Somehow my family, friends, and caching friends managed to co-ordinate visiting so despite being in a hospital about forty miles from home, I had visitors every day.

I was discharged from hospital after five weeks but there were lots of things I couldn't do. I couldn't look after myself so I wasn't able to go home. It was rather frustrating not even being able to lift the kettle to make a drink. I stayed with friends and I continued to have regular visitors.

After fifty-nine days with no geocache finds, I was taken out by one of my close caching friends and we found four caches... hooray, I was back!

I continued to have a slow but steady recovery and I eventually moved back home where I was reunited with my ever-faithful, friendly dog. I was taken out on regular caching trips and, over time, regained strength and confidence. A couple of my close caching friends organized a geocaching event in my honor - *'A MOOooooving Return'*. That meant I was officially back! There was a great turnout and it was so nice to see so many friends.

Over two years later, I am now able to drive, work, and get out caching, though I don't do much on my own and I'm pretty scared of cows! To get to this point I received physiotherapy, occupational therapy, hydrotherapy, and geocaching therapy! All of these have been instrumental in my recovery but the help, care, and support given to me by the geocaching community has just been so amazing.

# Gentle Icelandic Sheep

K.L. Allendoerfer
*karenlona*

I didn't notice the sign for Krysuvikurkirkja, but we must have passed it. It was our first time geocaching in Iceland. Tooling along in the old Toyota Corolla we had rented at Keflavik airport, my husband Gw0143 was at the wheel, and I had other things to occupy my mind: namely, charging the devices. In that car, the "cigarette lighter" was really meant to be a lighter. Our adapter thingy plugged into that slot, but it only seemed to work if Gunna—a poltergeist haunting one of the local geysers--was in a good mood. And she usually wasn't.

"It's an old church," Gw0143 said. "Or it used to be. The cache page says it burned down."

I promised our son that his Nintendo DSi was next in the charging queue, and we needed the other adaptor slot for the GPS charger. The iPods would have to wait. I twirled the adaptor cords around, holding them out at just the right angle. The little red adaptor light popped on and stayed.

"How many more caches before dinner?" I asked. "Today, we've already swam in the Blue Lagoon—the Blaa Lonio--spelunked, and explored the abandoned fishing village.

Yesterday, we rode ponies."

"Gentle Icelandic Ponies!" our son exclaimed (caching name Mr. Find-it-All) from the back seat.

"Yes, gentle Icelandic ponies," I agreed. "Today has been a lot of driving around, and these roads aren't that great, especially in this weather."

My raincoat, which was once a bright lime green, was dingy and bedraggled. For most of the trip, I'd been wearing a pair of Mary-Jane-style walking shoes that I had hoped would be versatile enough to take me from the hiking trail to the restaurant table. But they turned out to be more stylish than waterproof.

"It's sunny today," said Gw0143. "For the first time. We should take advantage of that and find as many caches as we can while the sun is shining!"

"Nooooo!" called Mr. FIA. "The sun doesn't go down here until 10:30 at night!"

"Eleven," said G, with what he seemed to think was a playful, mischievous smile.

The sun was shining on what looked to me like the treeless landscape of an alien planet. It was greener there than it was on the haunted part of the Reykjanes peninsula, with grass stretching out pleasingly across a flat open prairie until it climbed and softened the craggy mountains, some of them partially shrouded in fog. Whitish specks were scattered around the prairie; a few even visible on the hillsides.

"Can we go back to the ponies?" asked Mr. FIA.

"Those aren't ponies," said our daughter (caching name, The Purple Hippo), rolling her eyes without looking up from her iPod.

"They're sheep! Gentle Icelandic sheep. Isn't that cool?" exclaimed Gw0143, a bit too loudly.

"Not really," said TPH.

"Yes, let's see as much as we can while the weather is good. But I'm starting to get hungry," I added. "And my face is itchy. That mud in the Blaaaaaaaaa Lonio must not have agreed with my skin."

"Blaaaaa!" yelled Mr. FIA from the back seat.

"Here's where the church used to be," said G, pulling up to a random area of prairie and stopping.

"Ugh! You stop the car and the chargers all stop. Then when we start driving I have to get them working again, and by the time I do, you stop again. This is insane."

G didn't answer, just opened the car door and got out. He had his DeLorme GPS, so I took the Garmin out of the car—which was almost fully charged by then—and changed it from auto to pedestrian mode.

"Those sheep are too close," said Mr. FIA, indicating two sheep through the window that were, indeed, close enough for us to observe that they really weren't particularly cute or cuddly. One's fur was off-white, the other's off-gray. Their fur wasn't matted or obviously dirty, but I had no urge to pet them. They had horns curling back from their foreheads. "Can I stay in the car?" he asked.

"No," said Gw0143. "We're all going to look for this one. There have been a few DNFs so I need your help, everybody. It says something about the cache being under a stone . . . This way!" He turned around and started walking away from the sheep, down a path toward a weathered fence. Mr. FIA got out and followed him. There was a small, white cross sticking out of the ground.

It took a while for the Garmin to zero in on the cache zone after I unplugged it from the charger and switched modes. I got out and watched the little car icon moving around on the screen.

"I think the sheep-ies are cute," the Purple Hippo remarks, as she too got out of the car.

I nodded, slowly. "I suppose. Sheep are one of the few things they raise in Iceland that you can eat. That or fish. I don't like fish."

"They're excited to see us. I don't think they see many humans."

"Really?" I said. "I don't think they're excited. They might be scared. But you're right: no other humans for miles."

There was something lonely and a little sad about the peeling white fence with its gate to nowhere, the informational signage about a building that no longer existed, guarded by a flock of desultory, shepherd-less sheep. Oh, and then there was the fact that it was on a volcanic island in the middle of the ocean! Even the sun didn't dispel the feeling that we were the last Hobbits in Middle Earth.

The entire site of where the church used to be was marked by a field of stones. Gw0143 and Mr. Find-it-All were there, turning the stones over, one by one. The Purple Hippo went over to join them.

The stone-search didn't look promising to me, or fun. And the GPS said we were still off by 40 feet.

Staring at the little screen on the Garmin, I followed the GPS car icon as I walked to one side of the church foundation, near what might have been its entrance, marked by a post. I kept my eyes glued to the Garmin's screen as I walked in a straight line, and the distance number grew smaller. There was a hole next to the post, and in that hole was a rock. I squatted down to pick up the rock, and under it was a flash of blue plastic. The plastic looked like the cap of a 15-mL Falcon tube that I might use in the lab. And in fact, it was exactly that. It was the cache! A Falcon tube enclosed in a protective sleeve! I pulled it out and stood up, yelling "I found it!"

That's when I felt the presence of someone right in front of me, sharing in my find. I looked up into the eyes of... a brown-ish sheep. We stared at each other for a long moment, and then it turned and ran, first toward the other members of the family, and then off into the grass. I watched its tail bounce up and down as it bounded away. I realized I was breathing hard, and I could feel my heart beating.

"What? Did you find it?" called Gw0143 from the church foundation site. "I was about to DNF it."

"Just followed the coordinates," I said. "But that sheep seemed to have been guarding it. He surprised me. I guess I surprised him too!"

We signed the log and I posed for a picture, holding the tube in one hand and the log and pencil in the other. My First Geocaching Encounter with a Sheep!

"Mom, you know your face is really red!" TPH pointed out. I checked it in the car's rear view mirror as we drove away, before wrestling with the chargers again. She was right again. It wasn't just the reflection off my girly pink Red Sox hat, or the contrast with my jaunty lime-green raincoat. My face was radiating its own redness. Only I would get sunburned in Iceland!

Chargers plugged in, I finally got another chance to read the pamphlet from the hotel about local things to do. I checked if there is anything to say about the church. It turned out that the church had burned down only recently, in 2010. And it was built in 1857. It was no ancient Viking ruin. But I was still glad we had gone.

The shadows were lengthening as I entered an address for a restaurant into the GPS.

When we got there, it served a wide variety of menu items. It was mostly seafood, but I ordered the lamb. And it was delicious.

# A Tick A Tack

Keely McGrew
*justkeely*

My family took a sojourn into the West Coast wilderness a few years ago. On our minds were finding "grandfather caches" (one of the hundred oldest active caches) and the wild west coast scenery. We wanted to rejoice in the mountains, hike in the hills, revere in seascapes, and find inspiration in northwest waterfalls. We did all of that and more, but our first mission was to conquer GC78, "Firestone," the 43rd oldest active Geocache in the world, and the second oldest active cache in California.

In order to get there, we drove north on 101 from San Francisco through the Muir Woods and then into the Mt Tamalpais Park. It was a beautiful drive and we could have stayed there forever. The scenery started to change from dark, surrealistic woods to rolling hills of straw-colored grasses dotted with trees as we got closer to the parking for the trail to the cache.

It says in the cache description that it is a relatively flat, "easy and relaxing" walk from the trailhead. I think that is true if one does not have small children with them, particularly children who are a little clumsy yet in their walking. Even though my youngest child with us was six and a real trooper, he was not always careful about where he put his feet. This made for a nerve-wracking hike. Although the trail is relatively flat, it is narrow, and follows along ridges and hillsides that angle off to the right in uncertain angles, so that one slip of foot and loss of balance would send one down the hill and potentially into head-bashing rocks or trees or stumps. Most of the hike consisted of either my husband or I walking right behind our little one, counseling him to watch his step, holding our breaths, and prepared to intervene if he fell.

Very early on in the walk, we encountered some large birds flying about, ahead of us and some distance away. I spied one with the binoculars close up, before our little guy scared him away through his thumping footfalls and chattering, and I am fairly certain what we were seeing were golden eagles. It is still debatable, but I did read that the Mt Tamalpais area, where we were, has the highest ratio of nesting golden eagles in the world.

All told, we were out there for about 1.5 hours, and we estimate that our hike was round trip about three miles. We seemed to have parked a good distance from the cache, and then the trail made a surprising number of turns before we finally arrived at the cache site. It was not necessarily hot out there (the west coast being a lot cooler than we even expected it to be), but the sun was mercilessly shining down on us the whole time.

The last hundred or so feet of this hike was the hardest for us, and my oldest swore I was trying to kill him. The youngest was very thirsty. Plus, for some reason, my husband had led us a harder way back to parking that involved walking up a terrible hill. But the true terrible effects of the hike were just starting to show themselves, in the form of small red-brown scurrying creatures that were just starting to make their ascent up our bodies.

The first tick revealed itself on the youngest child's leg when we got to the car. It was his first experience with ticks, which is surprising, since we live in an area where deer ticks are prevalent in the woods, but perhaps this is because he usually opts to stay behind with grandparents when we hike far enough into the woods to encounter them.

I told him what it was, and killed it and removed it from him. He must have misunderstood what I said, because for some reason he thought I called it a "tack." Maybe it was my Texas accent!

For the next three to six hours, we continued to experience crawling reminders of this cache as they rose up to bite us in the metaphorical (or perhaps literal) butt.

They must have either really liked my youngest, or had fallen into the folds of his jeans, or maybe it was just the fact that he was smaller and closer to the edges of the dried, wheat colored grasses that lined the trail, but he was definitely the greatest victim. He was also the most terrified of these things of anyone I have ever seen. He might have an actual phobia of ticks. My husband and I were finding them on us occasionally and would silently pull them off, squeeze them, and throw them out the window. Every time the little one would spy another crawling up his leg, or along the seat near him, he would start screaming, "A TACK! A TACK!" and we would have to pull over, get out, open his door, and kill the offending creature and get rid of it. This went on for hours, and we were so over it.

Possibly the adrenaline rush of being scared, or perhaps car-sickness from the long and winding way up Highway 101 had this little one now telling us to pull over because he was going to be sick, and puking on pull-outs for the rest of our drive.

Needless to say, this experience detracted from our overall satisfaction with the day, and actually changed our plans for the night, as we ended up stopping early and getting a hotel room instead of claiming our camping reservations in the Redwood Forest so we could strip the boys down, check them for ticks, shake out their clothing, shower them, and let the little one recover from his terrible Tick-A-Tack.

# Leopards, Ducks, and Cher

Kurth Warren
*KurRae*

My name is Kurth, and my wife's name is Raenae. We go by the handle "KurRae" in the geocaching world. We are not experts by any means. We generally just try to have fun, and that was our goal for this day's hunt.

We started at the truck, and headed toward the cache (GC12ZN1) "Half of the Half." Getting to it would only be half of the fun!

Once I crossed the road, I turned and noticed that my son Steven, twenty-one years of age at the time, was walking like he was wearing flippers. He was actually waddling, like a duck. I giggled and asked him what was wrong. He stated that his shoes were messed up, and he looked to me for help.

Steven has Down Syndrome, so even though he is old enough to legally drink, he has the mental capacity of a young teen. He is a rather large boy for his height, standing about five and a half feet tall. He would often state that he, "wants to be skinny like Grandma." So we decided to take him geocaching to get out of the house and start walking off some of those "not so Grandma pounds," as he would say.

This was Steven's first experience geocaching, and as it turned out, our adventures that day would take us on an unexpected route: a fun and exciting one.

Laughing with Steven and his Mother after realizing that he had on shoes that were almost four sizes too big, we decided to head back to town and buy some shoes. We arrived in Lander, Wyoming a few minutes later. The first store stop proved to be a no-go, and we would spend the next couple hours looking all over town for a pair of shoes that fit him. On the last stop, I decided to stay in the truck and figure out which caches we should go for next.

Steven came out of the store bouncing and smiling. His Mother came out shaking her head and laughing quietly. At first I thought he had found a pair of shoes that were camouflage. Boy was I wrong. He opened the truck door and stuck up his left foot. "Look at what I got." He said.

I laughed, "What are those?"

"My cat shoes." He said as he climbed into the back seat.

"Those are the only shoes they had in his size." Raenae said as she flipped the seat back and climbed in.

I turned around and leaned over the seat to look at his shoes a little closer. They were leopard printed girl shoes, loafers! I looked up at him to see a wide cheesy grin on his face.

"What?" He asked.

"Those are girl shoes."

"Yup!" He said folding his arms and sticking out his chin. "My girls. I love Cher."

Wondering what Cher has to do with the shoes? Well, it's like this: Steven's Grandpa likes Cher's music. It was his Grandpa's shoes he had on before, and since the subject of Grandpa was fresh on his mind, he associated the girl shoes with Cher and his love for teasing Grandpa about her.

"Cher my girl, my shoes, Grandpa stays away!" He said and started laughing.

His laughter is contagious, and I turned around smiling to start the truck. We stopped for some lunch and then headed back out to the "Half of the Half" cache.

Steven took the lead on the trail toward the cache in his new leopard print loafers. Only stopping when the trail would divide, he would wait for me to tell him which direction to go. About halfway up the trail, I noticed that he was humming a tune. I looked at Raenae and asked her if she knew what song he was humming. She had no idea. So I asked him.

"Time." He said. "You know," He started humming and twirling his hands and snapping his fingers. "Turn time," he turned around and started walking again. "Back and find way." He sang on.

We laughed as we realized that he was singing "Turn back time" by (of course) Cher.

We finally made it to the cache and Steven found it right away. It was a good cache, and it had some good swag in it. We did our thing and explained to Steven that we had to trade items and sign the logbook. He didn't want to sign the book at first, but I believe that he eventually did. He wanted to trade for a fishing lure that was in the cache, so we did. We placed the cache back and headed for the truck.

Off to a new cache! In the back seat, I could hear Steven singing along with some sort of hip hop music he had on his IPod. We decided to find another cache that wouldn't be too hard for him to get to, but one that required him to do some walking. So we set out for cache (GC2A0JC) "Lizard Hide," with a little higher terrain rating than the last one.

We found the cache and did our business. The hike to the cache was uneventful, unless you count our gawking at the surrounding scenery. It was beautiful out, and the temperature was just right for such a hike. The hike back to the truck would turn out to be a bit more.

About halfway back to the truck, Steven stopped and started to complain about his feet. I knew that the shoes they had bought would end up being trouble. So we did the only thing we could. Luckily Steven had put his Grandpa's shoes in my backpack. So he donned the larger shoes and we set off again.

The closer we got to the road, the more people we started to see. Steven was once again walking like he had on flippers. So instead of letting him look foolish by himself, we created a game.

My wife and I began walking like ducks, too! The people who saw us smiled and passed by with some laughter. At least Steven didn't think that they were laughing at him. Oh no ... he thought they were laughing at me, because I was the one making duck noises and funny faces as we began to race the closer we got to the truck!

Steven had a blast on his first geocaching experience. Since then, he has gone with us to some events and he has made some new friends. Now when he goes with us, he tries to race us to the caches. Every now and then, he even finds them without the use of a GPS (after it gets us close, I mean).

And the moral of the story: we always make sure we have an extra pair of shoes that will fit him nicely and that his IPod has Cher on it! We don't always race back to the truck or the minivan walking like ducks, but we do make sure that Cher is there waiting for him on his iPod.

# Adventures with Zombies

Dawn Thieme
*gemini76*

It was a very early start to the day, in anticipation
of the upcoming event. As the excitement built, I hadn't gotten
much in the way of sleep. After getting out of bed, I got
dressed, ate my now-traditional donut and orange juice
breakfast, and then got in my car and headed north. I met up
with Michael (Irishflea) in York, and we departed for Omaha
for the Zombie Apocalypse Event for Geocachers!

He'd woken early, he said, to get ready. He said his makeup
took forever, but the costume was easy. I could see why;
Michael looked like he'd been shot in the face a few times.
Blood oozed down his chin and goatee. His brains were
crawling out of his head. He wore a long-sleeve shirt that was
ripped and bloody, and ripped jeans. I, on the other hand,
looked very dead, thanks to my mask. I wore plain black, and
my skin was greenish-gray, with a sunken, skeletal-looking
face, and long, stringy, matted hair. (I didn't put my mask on
until we got to the event, so I needed makeup underneath.)

We arrived an hour early, so we thought we'd grab a few
caches that were located near the event location. While we were

doing that, Michael got a call from his cousin, Jim (Jimmy63), saying that he was at Hy-Vee and would be attending the event as well. He was dressed as zombie hunter in hunter orange. (Cool!)

The purpose of the event, Zombie Apocalypse, A Thriller of an Event (GC62EN8)¬, hosted by geocachers J&LA, was to earn as many infection points as possible. Some of the tasks the teams (ours was Jim, Michael and myself) were challenged with were things like holding an ammo can, chasing a muggle's child, holding a baby, or using a photo booth to snap some selfies. We didn't get to do those, or to sing "Staying Alive" or to dance to "Thriller," but we did have a very quick tour of Omaha, and got beat by the other team.

But we had fun, anyhow. We went to a hospital, the Bohemian and West Lawn cemeteries, a morgue and two mausoleums. We did a snapshot in front of a marquee with a specific time of 12:22 (and finding one that showed the time wasn't as easy to find as we thought it would be), and one on a bus stop bench. We saw a black cat and a kitten, and of course, had to take photographs with both of them. Another of our goals was to get people to honk at us on the corner of 72nd and Dodge. When we got back to Hy-Vee, I donned my Husker sweatshirt, as we needed 'Husker' gear, too!

After returning to the event location, even though we weren't even close to winning the contest, we had an absolute blast, and the hosts were nice enough to let everyone log a shared FTF for the event! Oh, and we all had cupcakes! As the event was winding down, everyone decided to start working on another puzzle from J&LA to be retrieved at a later date. It was a nice challenge, and really got our brains thinking. Not an easy task being a zombie!

After the event and before heading to a trail for our next caches, we said goodbye to Jim and our fellow cachers, then stopped at Burger King for a quick bite to eat. There were a few customers who stared, but it was pretty quiet overall, as it was after the noon-time rush.

We then headed toward Ashland to get the GCF trail logged, even though we arrived later than intended. As we were caching along, there was this lady who kept looking at us from her car, like we were crazy (Michael was still in zombie attire at this point), and he tried to explain to her what geocaching was all about. She drove off, but then a mile or so down the road, there she was again. He tried again to tell her what geocaching was, but once again drove off. I guess she really didn't want to know what we were doing, after all, despite her curiosity! (I thought this was funny. If he were really a zombie, wouldn't I have been the first one he'd attacked?)

Probably a half hour or so later, both a city and county officer pulled us over (we were already stopped, as there was a cache nearby), and they basically told us they had received a phone call about someone looking like a zombie, or at the very least, a very suspicious person! (It was funny that they didn't mention either the 'hand' sticking out of the back of the trunk, or the fake skeleton in the back seat!) They let us go, thankfully, or I wouldn't be writing this story.

By then, we only had a few more caches to get, so we finished up with that right as the sun began to set and took the long way back to Omaha through backroads and small towns neither of us knew existed. It was a wonderful and awesome day, and we made a lot of new friends and memories!

# Discovering Geocaching

Ralph Schuessele
*res2100*

Like so many other geocachers, geocaching has greatly influenced my life and has brought me much enjoyment since I first discovered it in 2002.

Trying to find something to do with my five-year-old son Tylor, a friend told me about the Bruce Trail that was close to where we live, so I started seeking them out. After starting out late one day, and having discovered a few portions of the Bruce Trail, my son and I were out hiking another section down an unfamiliar trail in an area known as Speyside. The trail started out through a thick forest, which soon became an open field and then continued on back into another wooded and rocky area on the Niagara Escarpment. We came across a few forks along the trail, randomly chose a path, and continued on enjoying our adventure.

After over an hour of exploring the trail with my son, I soon realized that we had gone quite far. I also knew that the sun would be setting in just over an hour, and at this point, we did not know where we were as it was all so new to us. We had no food or water, and no flashlight. We could turn back knowing we would find the car, but what if we didn't make it back before it got dark? I started to get worried, but didn't want to worry my son. My thought was that if we kept walking, we would eventually come to a road and easily follow it back to where we had parked. However, that never happened.

We continued walking, following unfamiliar trails, and then we came across something familiar-looking ... the open field we had previously hiked through. We had hiked in a loop, and it was then that I knew where we were. We were maybe only 15 minutes from where we had parked! I was relieved we had made it out safely just as the sun was setting.

Having enjoyed hiking various sections of the Bruce Trail over the past month with my son, I didn't want us to get lost on the trail again during our next outing, so I looked online for more information about the Bruce Trail, and I came upon a post about geocaching. I had never heard of geocaching before, as it was still a very new activity in 2002. As I read the post, I thought it sounded intriguing, so I went to the geocaching website and created an account. I decided I wanted to try it and looked into getting a GPS, and bought a Magellan SporTrak Pro online.

When the GPS arrived, I couldn't wait to try geocaching, so when my son got home from school that day, along with my mother, the three of us went off to find our first cache a couple kilometers from home. It was the 2nd closest cache to home, one of only 401 caches at the time within 160 kilometers of home. We headed down the local trail into the valley and along the river. The GPS then pointed us to go back up the hill, so we did, and wound up at the fallen tree on the hillside. There it was: a round cookie tin filled with various items and a log book. Mom had found it while my son and I were searching a bit higher up. We made our first trades, and wrote about our adventure in the log book, and then again on the cache listing at home. We had found our first cache, Silver Creek Find (GC2EF3), on November 6, 2002. From this point on, we were hooked on geocaching.

The next day after school, we went again to find the other cache in town, and then the day after that we had to go much further to find a couple more caches. I wanted to go out more and more for caching and exploring the world around us. Our third find would take us to a very neat geological place called the Cheltenham Badlands. This would also become the place where I placed my first Earthcache, Cheltenham Badlands Earthcache (GCNXFF ), a few years later, and which would become one of the top favorited caches in Ontario.

Not only was finding caches so much fun, I also decided to hide my first cache a few weeks later, and would hide my first five caches over the next couple of months. My first hide was a three stage multi called Please Water The Flowers (GCAF17) in a local cemetery and it is still active today after over 13 years. The First to Find of my first hide was the top cacher in Ontario at the time with over 300 finds and he had driven 80km to find my cache. I felt honored.

Along with finding caches comes not finding them, and the day after hiding my first cache and after 30 finds, I got my first DNF (did not find). The cache we couldn't find was hidden by the same top cacher who had found my first hide. The cache we couldn't find was Millenium Boardwalk (GC5769) which was located on the beaches of Lake Ontario.

After finding a few caches during the day, I had called up a friend and asked him if he wanted to go find a couple of caches in the evening. We had quite the adventure finding one, and then the next we spent a good hour or more on the beach searching for the elusive micro. In the dark, we searched the sand, the gardens, the trees, the rocks ... everywhere we could think of, but just couldn't find it and had to give up in the end making it my first ever DNF. It felt like a failure not being able to find it.

A couple weeks later, we were once again in the area and I called up my friend to give this cache another try and we once again went to search for it at night, but had a small hint of where to look this time. This time we found it! It was a film container under the cover of a lamp post. We never would have ever thought to lift up the base cover of a lamp post. It felt really wrong to do that at the time, but it is something that has become very common as the years went on.

It took me 81 days to find my first 100 caches, and I found 678 caches in my first year of caching. The past 13+ years has been filled with many firsts, such as meeting another cacher on the trails for the first time a month and a half after starting caching, to attending our first ever event GHAGAFAP II (GCGBR9) ten months later and even becoming the first cacher in Canada to find 1000 caches. We even made our first geocoin in 2005, and was also fortunate to own the first Geocache with a 7-digit GC code, GC10000 - A New Beginning.

Geocaching has brought us so much enjoyment over the years. It has taken us on many adventures, given us awesome memories and helped us make many friendships that will last a lifetime. This all happened because my son and I got lost one day while hiking along the Bruce Trail.

# The Last Gift, My First GPS

Lenore Dressel
*DresselDragons*

My first GPS was a grey Lowrance iFinder. It was the last personal item my father had given to me when he became sick in 2005. He was diagnosed with Silicosis - scarring of his lungs caused by breathing in tiny bits of silica in his work environment. Over the course of a year, I watched my dad struggle as it became harder and harder for him to breathe, eventually becoming tethered to an oxygen concentrator.

I am sure his illness was frustrating for him. It was not that he could not go places - he had a portable oxygen concentrator. But it became harder and harder to go anywhere. Excursions for him switched from fishing and boating to doctor visits. It is a sad day when an avid outdoorsman can no longer do the things he enjoys to do outdoors.

His gift of the GPS was more than simply an electronic device. It also allowed me to reconnect to my love of the outdoors, something I had forgotten, and to share that with my father during his final year.

My husband already owned a GPS: a little yellow eTrex. My family found our first Geocache with it. I don't know if it was the GPS or user (me), but I thought that GPS was rather hard to use. So, there is a 3 month gap between our first cache find, using the Garmin, and the second cache find, using the Lowrance iFinder. Looking back, I don't know if the iFinder was really was easier to use than the Garmin, or not. I think I was more motivated to use the "new" GPS, to do things that my father no longer could.

My daughters and I began geocaching more frequently after we received the iFinder. In essence, we became my father's travel bugs. We would find geocaches and report our adventures to him. He enjoyed the stories of our hikes in the woods, finding a playground that we never knew existed, getting lost down some back country road while trying to navigate to a cache, and the trinkets we would bring home. I took a lot of pictures to share with him.

We also released our first travel bugs into the wild! As they travelled, we had more stories to share with my dad. Although he enjoyed our stories, you could tell he wished he could join us.

I eventually purchased a new red faceplate for the iFinder after losing it in the woods while caching. I had a belt holster for the GPS and a 2-year old. That was not a good combination. Many of my hikes eventually involved carrying my daughter. One day, a well-placed toddler foot kicked off the GPS while in search of a multi-stage Geocache. I was so worried that I lost the iFinder forever, but my 30-minute search for it was successful. This experience yielded 3 results: 1) a new faceplate that is easier to spot on the ground, 2) replacement of the holster with a lanyard, and 3) another story to share with my dad.

I do not remember the first geocoin that we brought home to show him. It was probably a Greenman or USA geocoin. I only remember his reaction. As a former coin collector, he was enthralled, especially when I told him that Geocachers were designing their own coins and using them as a personal trade items to leave in Geocaches. This was when I began collecting geocoins. Now, not only did I have stories of the Geocaches we were finding to share with him, but I was also bringing over my latest geocoin purchases and trades to show him.

Eventually, I even decided to mint my own geocoin. I knew it was another experience that I could share with my dad. Once I had the artwork completed, I rushed it over to share with my dad. I don't know who was more excited, him or me.

My father died a year and a half after he gave me the iFinder. There were so many stories I could no longer share with him. He never got to see our completed geocoin, or hear how we eventually won the GPS that eventually replaced the iFinder.

I never stopped caching; it became my therapy. Each time I looked down at the iFinder while hiking, I felt I was taking a walk in the woods with my dad.

Eventually, the iFinder did not work well, and had to be retired. It still rattles around in a drawer; I could not bear to throw it away, reminding myself that it was the final gift from my father. However, looking back now, I do not think the iFinder was his last gift. It was just a tool that allowed me to reconnect with outdoors, and instill a love of the outdoors in my children, and that is a far greater gift.

# Diamond Studded Geocache

Ginny Grudzinski
*Ginny & Stevecat*

Two of our young grandchildren came to spend a weekend with my husband and me. The first evening, they begged to stay up all night. We promised them if they'd go to sleep, we'd take them on their first geocaching adventure in the morning.

To sweeten the deal, I also read them a bedtime story. I was in the middle of working on my novel, a geocaching adventure, so I read an excerpt from it to them. The part of the story I shared was when the robbers hid some diamonds in the hollow of a tree. I described the scene and the area in great detail, and they soon fell asleep, I'm sure dreaming of the adventure that awaited them.

The next day, we drove to the first cache location. We walked through the wooded area and came to the clearing. We showed the kids that the GPS was indicating that we were within about twenty feet of the cache.

My little granddaughter's eyes widened when she saw the tree. "This is it!" she cried. "This is the tree where the robbers hid the diamonds!"

I looked around and sure enough, it was very much like the description in my story. There were two downed logs that formed an "x," and three large trees side-by-side, each with its own hallow. "It's in the center tree," she proclaimed.

We found the cache, which coincidently was in the center tree, and signed the log, letting them sign their newly minted geocaching name.

Then, they looked through the swag, and my granddaughter was clearly very disappointed. "Where are the diamonds?" she demanded.

"Honey, that was just a story," I tried.

She shook her head, her little red pigtails flying, "No," she insisted, "I know they are here, go back and look again, Nani, they have to be here!"

I looked again, and even lifted her up and let her look for herself, but no diamonds. There was nothing else in that or any of the other trees, but she would not be dissuaded.

Finally, my husband winked at me and said, "Ok, let's go back to the Jeep, and Nani will do another search for the diamonds."

*Okay*, I thought. *What could it hurt to just play along?*

My husband managed to herd them back to the Jeep, and I pretended to make a thorough search of the location. I knew I had some crystal beads at home so I said, "Yep, I grabbed a few of the diamonds. I'll give them to you when we get back home." She was happy with that and we continued our geocaching.

We did a few more caches, where they enjoyed the hunt and happily traded swag, and soon forgot about the Diamond tree, until we arrived home. We pulled into the driveway and my granddaughter immediately asked, "As soon as we get in the house, can we see the diamonds?"

Yikes, I hoped she'd forgotten!

I quickly (while my husband distracted them) went to my craft room and pulled out a handful of clear Swarovski crystals, put them in a little bag and slipped them in my backpack. When we unloaded the pack she marveled at the diamonds, holding each one up to the light. She quickly put them on a string and wore them as a necklace, very proud of her find.

But that evening we went out for dinner and she looked so worried. "Nani," she whispered, "What if the robbers see me with the diamonds? Will they come after me?" She tucked her pretty necklace in her shirt, but the worry didn't leave her face.

We tried to assure her that it was ok, that it was really just a story, and the diamonds were just beads I had; she had nothing to worry about. But since the cache location was so much like the description in the story, and I had produced a bag of "diamonds," nothing could allay her fears.

Finally, we went home and decided to tell her the ending of the story. I quickly made up the final scene where the robbers could not remember where they left the diamonds. They could not remember if it was in a tree, or under a rock, or somewhere else. In fact, they were not even sure what state they were in when they hid them.

She looked less worried, but just to be sure I told her the robbers were caught and put in prison, and they would never be back for the diamonds again.

Finally assured that the "diamonds" around her neck were safe, she relaxed.

But before bedtime she asked again, "Are you sure the robbers can't remember where the diamonds are?"

"Yes honey, I'm sure."

"Are you sure they won't be back?"

"Yes, very sure."

"And you're sure no one will come look for the diamonds?"

"Yes, absolutely sure."

She jumped out of bed, grabbed her shoes and cried, "Then let's go back and get the rest of them!"

# Summer Fun

Dasmonda Allen
*SouthernGrits*


It was June 2014, and my step-daughter Ashley was
coming to visit. We hadn't seen her in two years, though we
talked as much as possible on the phone. We were SO excited!
Since I had last seen her, I had taken up geocaching again,
thanks to my son Zakkary (AFBLUETHUNDER), and I
couldn't wait to introduce her to the game. When she came, I
did just that.

The first cache we went to was "Another Rides the Bus"
(GC37ATJ). Ashley made the find and posted her log: "Found
on a training mission/session with SouthernGrits and the little
one. =)." The second cache was after a family dinner. Ashley
posted "Found on another training mission with Southerngrits
and the little one. This one has apparently been moved, so said
trainer had to locate it again as well." She continued to cache
with me on and off during her visit and would eventually log a
total of 18 caches over the course of two weeks (although I am
sure she missed at least one log during our trip to Carlsbad).

The last cache that we logged together before she boarded
her plane home was "The World's Largest Equestrian"

(GC3N2R6) on June 19, 2014. She and her youngest brother Mark (LilRainier1) went for the smiley as I stayed with the car, just a few yards away, in the cell phone waiting area. Lil' One showed her how to be stealthy in an airport parking lot and come up with the container. Little did I know that would be our last cache together.

In September 2015, we lost Ashley due to injuries resulting from a car accident. She was only 18, had just started college, and had many dreams of returning to Washington one day. It would be 18 months or so before I actually read any of her posted logs, but when I did, they brought a much needed smile to my face.

We made the trip from New Mexico to Missouri where she lived with her mom and step-dad to say our final goodbyes.

Each day we were there, I took a quick look on the geocaching app to see if there were any nearby. I wanted to show Ashley's mom and boyfriend what she was always talking about. But alas, none were close enough to grab in the midst of sorrow and chaos. I checked by the hotel, by her work, by the house, by the funeral home … nothing.

On the day of the funeral, we had tons of family and friends around us. Ashley definitely packed the house! Lots of tears, laughter and stories were shared. A dove was released, and then it was time.

As grandparents departed with our other children, we parents took Ashley on her final ride. Her mom, dad, step-dad and I followed the hearse to the crematorium about a half hour away. We took care of the final arrangements and then stepped outside for a moment of weird relief. We had made it through all the arrangements, visitations, stories and sorrow … and there hadn't been a single not one fight. We had worked as a team.

I decided to take one last look at my app to see if a cache was close by. AMAZINGLY, there was one just on the other side of the parking lot. I looked at my husband and told him I was taking a walk. With cell in hand, he knew exactly where I was headed.

I circled the tree behind the drugstore several times. I knew it HAD to be here, but I was in town for a funeral, not caching. Thus, all I had to work with was my cell phone. The GPS kept bouncing. First I was 12 feet away, then seven, then 10. I'd look at the aerial imagery again and I was sure I had the right tree out of the few that were there. A simple park and grab my foot! Just as I walked around the tree again, I noticed I was behind a Walgreens. That was the company Ashley had worked for at the time of her passing. Weird coincidence? I wasn't sure, but just as I was about to give up, I decided to ask Ashley where it was. CRAZY thought, I know, but I did it. As I was walking deeper into the middle of the tree, in my dress clothes, I said "Awww, come on Ashley, I know you see it." (She always saw them.)

At that moment, my phone app honed in on the cache three feet away ... and stabilized there. "Ok, I'll look once more. Where is it?" I asked. As I was about to give up and walk back across the lot, something made me step back and take one more look. THERE IT WAS! I had checked that location a couple times; I was sure of it. But clear as day, there was a pill bottle hanging from a tree branch, at my eye level. I signed the log "SouthernGrits and angel Washingtonianatheart" and took a photo of both the log and the cache container. I smiled and thanked Ashley for her help from beyond. This was our first cache since her death. As I logged the cache on the app, it was then that I noticed the name of the cache:"Summer Fun"(GC572NA). Tears filled my eyes as it was all too fitting. We started caching together in the summer, and that was when we got to visit most often. Our best, and longest, conversations were in the summer on the back porch. My online log was "Found with my angel....Washingtonianatheart...by my side. RIP."

I walked back to the vehicle where the other three were still waiting and chatting. I shared with Ashley's mom what I had done and asked if she wanted to see what a geocache hunt was all about. She said she did, as Ashley had talked quite often about caching with me the previous summer. We walked to the tree again together and I explained to her my methodology and how I located the container ... right down to asking Ashley for help. She smiled, knowing Ashley was still with us. I showed her the log, and we replaced it as we had found it.

That would be the only cache I found in Missouri during that trip. But it was OH so perfect!

When I returned home, I started trying to figure out how to process everything. My geocaching friends were right there for me every step of the way. Moto*Joe even placed an ammo can up on the mountain for Ashley on his cacher's trail since she was involved in the game, if only for a brief time. I was able to tag along for the placement and personally placed an Elvis CD and a book inside to honor her love of reading and of the King. "The Pennsylvanian Trail/Washingtonianatheart" (GC68YX2) sits high on the mountain side overlooking the Alamogordo valley. I have also set up a travel bug for her on a silver angel ornament. The copy tag stays with me at all times on my keychain and eventually, I will release the actual angel travel bug into the caching community. Maybe her mom or boyfriend will take up the hobby and the travel bug will cross their paths. Until then, she travels with me in my caching pack.

I still remember the day that I got Ashley into geocaching, as she sat at the kitchen table trying to figure out what her trail name would be. She tried what seemed like a dozen different names to get "Washington" into it in some fashion. Finally, one idea worked and she forever became Washingtonianatheart. A fitting name for a lovely gal.

It has been almost nine months now since we lost Ashley. I have turned to geocaching now more than ever. It is more than a game to me; it is a much needed stress reliever. And when I can't locate a cache container, you bet I ask Ashley for help. RIP Washingtonianatheart.

# Walk with an Angel

Nathan Haworth
*PommiePirates*

**In 2010, my life experienced a huge DNF** when I lost my fiancée. Hours turned to days, the days turned to weeks, weeks turned to months and I was still lost and alone. My footsteps left no imprints. I was moving forward, and I couldn't go back. No matter where I went, I felt that I always ended up back at the beginning.

A new path was intended for me, but what was it? I began to wonder how my life was going to pan out, so I walked and walked, and gradually started to clear my head, exploring, challenging myself, and slowly but surely, wherever I went I started to feel She was watching over me, nudging me, guiding me. I started to find things, see things, numbers, words, and unexplainable coincidences. I started to feel. It was almost an embracing presence pointing me home. I didn't need to feel alone anymore.

Through the gloom and despair, I met my future wife who was walking her own path after losing her father. She brought me back through to the light, made my life worth living again. She gave me strength to help her with her demons, and we began to rebuild gradually. But we knew we needed to get away, to see the world. Furthermore, the love we had to take with us would allow us to share in our losses but live in our future, walking side-by- side.

We booked a ticket on the first plane out of the UK and started our new lives in Australia with our family down under. Geocaching was a much-needed distraction from the pain and gave us both moments of reflection; we came across many stories, happy and sad, and we soon came to realize that fellow cachers had similar experiences.

This opened a whole new world for my wife and I. We toured the East coast of Australia, and we yearned to travel even more. We took in countries like Vietnam, Cambodia and Kuala Lumpur. The captivating sights, sounds, smells, people and the occasional wrong turn en route to caches, always led us to adventure. Once, my wife even ended up cutting her leg pretty badly on some thorny bushes, and she now has a scar which she never lets me forget that I overlooked to read the waypoints. Even though I can see the lighter side to this accidental lapse in judgment, my wife still doesn't, but I now know to listen to my wife and realize that even though the GPS might say the cache is forward, always get the wife's approval and double-check if there's any waypoints beforehand.

Needless to say, we have shared in some amazing life changing moments together. Now, when planning our next caching journey, I wonder not what could have been but what will.

I knew my fiancée guided me in so many things. She was my angel, a compass steering me home. I know our path together has come to an end but her memory will not. No one ever truly leaves you, if their memory lives on. I released a Trackable My First Our First, a brief description of the angel who walked with me, guided me back. A path I now walk with my wife.

I wanted the memory of my fiancée to help others find their way, the way she helped me, a silent angel watching over others as they take their path through life, moving from cache-to-cache, person-to-person.

# Father Dragon, Baby Dragon

Koda Weir
*jack&berli*

## Firsts.

Our lives as GPS junkies are simply flourishing with" firsts"
because there are so many unique experiences, and finds, to be
had. But the "first" that means the most to me has little to do
with a physical container wrapped in duct tape. It has little to
do with location. It has to do with Jack. My dad. My partner in
crime. My fellow dragon. And although it might not seem that
my father qualifies for this challenge, our experience together
as geocachers has created one of the most valuable "firsts" in
my life.

I was a pretty messed up kid. There's no way to sugarcoat
how life has treated me. From the time I was twelve years old
to present. I suffered from - and still battle with - mental illness.
Now, at age twenty two, I often wonder how I am still alive.

My relationship with my dad was never very strong. I was
always either severely depressed or entirely too manic. I never
made time for my dad, and it was hard for him to make time for
me because it's hard to connect with a daughter who's so
unstable all the time. It's not like we had issues with each other;

we just weren't buddies. Through the turmoil of my teenage years, my dad was an excellent source of support, but we still had nothing in common... other than our love of nicknames.

In elementary school, I had decided that my name was far too girly, so my dad took to calling me Berli (almost as a joke) and in return I started calling him Jack. For some reason, the names stuck, and we used them so much that people often questioned why.

In 2013, we planned a trip to Point Reyes Lighthouse - just me and my dad. I remembered that there was a game called geocaching that I had been exposed to briefly years before. Out of curiosity, I checked the app store on my phone, and there it was. A geocaching app. The morning of our drive, I installed the app and created our account. Without a thought, we automatically signed up as jack&berli. We had a really nice day together and started our journey as geocachers.

In case you haven't figured out what my "First" is yet, I'll try to put it in words: geocaching gave my dad and I a first real reason to spend time together. It was our first common interest. It was the first thing that made us start talking with each other more. It was the first thing that gave us something to have inside jokes about. Geocaching gets the credit of our first selfies, and our first reason to get in the car and just drive.

I owe a lot to this game. It opened up a whole new world to us, and we have definitely evolved as cachers. We learned so much and so fast. In the beginning, as it is with all newbies I assume, we hacked at finding and hiding with such clumsiness. We learned to laugh at our mistakes and strove to be better every day. We also learned that more often than not, we had to put up with each other's moods and quirks. Dad started off with a bit more passion than I did, which often resulted in him finding caches while I sat in the truck grumpily waiting. But I had my good days too, where I was ready to set forth and conquer. As the months passed, I grew to look forward to our adventures more and more. I even started asking him to drive me to dance every evening so that we could cache on the way home. It wasn't long before other people started recognizing our name and associating it with tough hides.

Because of my obsession with dragons, we became known as the dragon whisperers. Adorable dragon images started popping up in the background of all our cache hide pages, and the words fire, wings, scales, claws, smoke, and lair became a regular part of our vocabulary.

Currently, and as of January 1st of 2016, Jack and I are working on a streak. We have found at least one cache every day so far this year. At times it can be a chore since where we live is pretty sparse, but we always make sure to meet our daily quota. We have often been stuck searching in the dark with flashlights, in the rain with umbrellas, or having to drive out of the way just to snag that one find. Yet every day ends in high fives in celebration of our success. Our goal is to reach one hundred days of finds in a row, and I think that we will make it no problem. Maybe we'll even make it to three hundred and sixty six days! Who knows?

In the end, geocaching is one of the coolest hobbies I've ever had. It takes me to places I've never been or would've never known about. It gets me out in nature, and has taught me to be a total stealth ninja. But most importantly, geocaching has made it possible for me to have a dad, for the first time ever.

# Kindred Geeks

Jennifer Anderson
*ColoradoJen1010*

If VeganGeekChic and I had met in high school, we would not have been friends. She was the cool girl I wanted to be and I was a nerdy, goody two shoes. We would not have thought we'd have any common ground. But somehow, life brought us to a point in our late twenties where our nerdy obsessions created that ground for us.

We originally connected over a shared lifelong obsession: books. We shared them, read them, discussed them and the movies that were made from them. An obsession we later developed and shared was geocaching. The excitement of the hunt, the thrill of a unique cache and the achievement of the elusive First to Find often had us giggling, jumping up and down and dancing around. We were beyond elated when it was announced that there were going to be library caches placed in all of the Denver Public Libraries. Since one of the perks of our jobs is that we can work from libraries, we decided to choose a different one each day. This way after we completed the work, we could begin the hunt for the cache.

Each cache was unique, and we liked and appreciated the

thought that was put into each puzzle and the construction of the cache itself. After we found each cache, we "nerded out" with the librarian about how cool libraries and caches were, and how thankful we were that they had allowed the placement of these caches. When the log was signed and the special code in the cache was recorded, we would decide where we would head the next day.

One particular morning dawned with Spring Perfection. VeganGeekChic and I were planning to take advantage of our Spring Break and do some geocaching. Our main objective was to head to the Valdez-Perry Library and complete our library challenge with GC5H1E5. Since we had found all of the active caches and retrieved all of the codes, now all that remained to do was to head to the library, sign the log and post the GC numbers for the caches we had found to meet the challenge.

As I was going about my morning, I got a very excited call from VeganGeekChic letting me know that the last library's cache had posted, Perfect Hiding GC5Q3A1. Our day had the possibility of being epic, as we could potentially get a First to Find on that cache and be the first to complete the series.

We read the description and determined we needed a black light. We apparently were bad geocachers, as neither of us had one nor could we find one no matter how hard we tried. We decided to head to the library and see if the black light app on VeganGeekChic's phone would be good enough.

As we stood outside the library waiting for it to open, we studied the other patrons trying to determine if they were muggles or cachers. Finally, the doors opened and we rushed forward like we were at a Black Friday sale. When no one else seemed as impatient to enter the library, we quickly determined that we were the only ones in "the know." However, we knew that Denver had a very active caching community with many First to Find hounds, so there was no telling how long we would be the only seekers.

We quickly found waypoint 1 and gathered the information we needed, then headed up the stairs. We began the search for waypoint 2, and experienced one of those moments where we thought we had found it, but we were a little nervous to tug on the container in case it wasn't the waypoint. Eventually, we tugged on it enough and determined that we had in fact found waypoint 2. The black light app helped our quest, and with a little effort, we were able to decipher it. Waypoint 3 was a little harder to find as it blended in fairly well. As we wandered back and forth, a nearby librarian could barely hide her glee. She gave a slight nod to indicate that we were in the right area. Having come so far it seemed that we might now be thwarted by an insufficient black light. While VeganGeekChic tried to work it out, I wandered around and found the final, much to the delight of that same giddy librarian. We decided to try our luck with the good old trial and error method, since we had the first 2 numbers of the combination. The librarian kept peeking her head around the corner to check on our progress. After many tries, we got it open and found the coolest log container ever! The librarian ran over to take our picture for the library website, which only slightly interrupted our dancing celebration.

With part one of our quest completed, we rushed to the next library. After completing the necessary calculations, we were able to locate the final and sign the log. We sank onto a nearby bench to log the find and include the list of caches that allowed us to complete the challenge.

The adrenaline started to leave our bodies and we began to feel the sinking feeling that comes with completing a task, and wondering what we would obsess about next. All of the sudden, both of our phones chimed to announce a text from our friend AaMb07. She excitedly told us to check out the Geocaching Colorado Facebook page. When we went to the page, we found that they had announced that the first 21 people to submit the hidden codes from the library caches would receive a special Geocoin, and the first to submit the correct codes would get their geocaching nickname engraved on the coin. We hurriedly got our codes ready and messaged them to the appropriate people. We were absolutely giddy, and kept laughing and smiling.

After a long wait, punctuated by much impatient checking of our phones and more giggling and dancing, it was finally confirmed that our codes were correct and they would be giving each of us an engraved First to Complete coin. Later that day, our picture was posted on the library website and we were able to share the heights of our geeky ecstasy with everyone, something neither one of us would have dared to do in those distant self-conscious high school days.

# Geocaching With Murphy

Grant Madden
*Pioneer 'n' Tiff*

## My name is Murphy. I'm a dog.

I'm into digging holes, naps, geocaching, and at night, I like to bark at the moon - for no particular reason. Typical yellow Labrador traits, no surprises there. Nevertheless, I have charm, especially with the Ladies.

I got people; they live inside the house at the front of the yard. At one time, I may have been Hers, but those days are gone. I am all His now. He's my first geocacher.   We took up geocaching not long after He stepped off a flight from Australia. He immigrated across three oceans to marry Her, and it was my responsibility to introduce him to the Northern Hemisphere. I was his first companion, from the day he arrived when he didn't know anyone. It was my cool charm that is responsible for Him geocaching.

He had been about a month or so before we started. He still had the traditional moving issues to deal with, so I didn't bother him that much. I just sat back and watched. However, I saw things, things that only a Dog with charm would see. Once She left the house to go to work, I could see it in His eyes. I saw him looking at the skyline with an inquisitive mind, and knew it would fall upon my four paws to broaden his world.

It was easy at first; we could walk to most of the local caches. But the walks began to get longer and longer as we moved further out into the world. And once He bought his own vehicle, complete with Dog seat belt, there was no stopping Us.

We like to hike, out on the trails tracing the steps of historians through the mountain terrain, crossing the desert like explorers, or following the trails left by the Missionaries around lakeside hills. I have my own backpack to carry my own food, water, and in case we meet some ladies, my own Travel Bug number to let them discover me.

In our adventures, we've found an abandoned Pony Express station, stood on active geological faults, traced extinct railway lines, and had a great time, because everywhere we went, it was always a first for him.

His First to Find in California: it was I who sniffed out the micro hidden in the bushes. The first benchmark recovery, I was digging at Ground Zero when We unearthed the covered disk. Even when He fell from the summit of Mount Seltzer and tore up his legs for the First Injury, I was there to drag Him back down the mountain to safety.

Being the First Dog at times has its drawbacks. One time in Hollywood when we stopped at a red light, some hot looking girls pulled up in a convertible beside us. They looked over and smiled at me; I wagged my tail and let the tongue hang out a bit more. They blew me a kiss; I planted a wet sloppy one on the window.

"Right back at ya babe."

That was His first time seeing my charm in action, but don't tell Her, or we will both be in the doghouse tonight.

We have been geocaching now for eleven years. I'm fourteen years of age and have a lot of great memories, but it's time for me to slow down. I'm enjoying retirement and don't take on any of the heavy hikes anymore … that's something I can leave to Him and one the Daughters. I still am invited to events though, and all the flashmobs.

We were in Balboa Park, San Diego earlier this year, just a

stone throw away from where the first World Wide Flash Mob was staged. I was there, at the very first flashmob that started it all, and remember the day. My picture was featured on geocaching.com and in the newspapers, so I still draw attention on the anniversary days. Especially from the ladies.

"Hey, who's that standing next to that good looking stud?"

My name is Murphy, I'm a dog, and this is Pioneer, my First Geocacher.

# Geocaching's Best Ambassador

Ginny Grudzinski
*Ginny & Stevecat*

The first time we told my mother-in-law, Pat, about geocaching, she thought we were crazy! "You're going to go hiking through the desert to find a Tupperware box that you don't even keep?" She didn't get it.

So when we told her we were taking an 18 state driving trip to go geocache, she thought we'd really gone off the deep end. But she agreed to come along, making sure we knew she was only there for the road trip; she didn't want anything to do with "that GPS game." That was fine with us; Steve's mom was in her 70's, and we cherished spending as much time with her as we could. Little did she know that was going to be her first geocaching trip!

Our first cache on the trip was at a rest stop. There were no hints, but the obvious place was a light post ... nope. Nothing there. We tried the gator next to it ... not there. Mom leaned out the motor home door and said, "I don't know how big this thing is you're looking for, but there's a couple of loose rocks near that boulder. I'll bet it's there." Sure enough, she'd found her first cache! We were excited, and she reluctantly agreed to sign the log.

The next time we stopped for a cache, she got out and searched with us, and while we the "experienced cachers" struggled to find it, she practically walked right up to it! Before long, she was hooked! And she had this incredible geo-sense. We'd stop for a cache, and before we could even get our bearings on the GPS, she'd have looked around and proclaimed, "Go up the path about 50 feet to that tree with pinecones, check for something hanging in the tree." Yep, it was there!

When we got back from the trip, we thought she'd gotten it out of her system, but hoped she'd at least go Geocaching with us on the weekends. She surprised us: she bought a GPS and had us load it with all the local caches. She was out and about almost every day!

She had so much fun, and her enthusiasm was contagious! We called her our Geocaching Ambassador! Everyone, and I do mean everyone she spoke with would hear about this wonderful game called geocaching.

She was at her doctor's office once, and through the course of the exam she told her Doctor about all the fun she was having with this game. We had a cache hidden in the parking lot of the medical center, so there, in the middle of her doctor's visit, mom and the doctor walked out to the parking lot and found it together!

She went to every geocache meeting and always sat by the door, greeting people, encouraging new geocachers, and sharing her knowledge of the game. Pretty soon, she was working on her streak of finding a cache every day of the year. We would stop to visit her on our way home from work and she'd either tell us of her day's geocaching adventure, or grab us and say, "I haven't gotten my cache today, let's go!"

She worked at it in earnest, and a few years later she had almost completed the, "Cache Every Day of the Year," grid with just a few scattered days left to go. She was determined to meet her goal, and nothing was going to stop her.

She had a routine medical procedure at the local hospital on one of those caching days, and as luck would have it there was a cache right across the street. Naturally, she wanted to get it first, in case the procedure took longer than expected. We quickly found the coordinates, but the cache was missing; we found the magnets but no container. There was no time to go look for another one, so we told her we'd contact the cache owner. If that was indeed where the cache was supposed to be, we'd replace it for them, and assured her we'd write her name on the log.

Her routine procedure turned out to be much more, and she ended up in open heart surgery. They lost her several times that evening, but the fine medical staff was able to resuscitate her. We stayed by her side waiting for her to wake up. The next day she roused, and we rushed to her bedside. She opened her eyes, looked up at us, smiled and asked, "Did you sign the log for me?"

She not only finished her caching streak, but she continued caching and telling everyone about geocaching. When walking became difficult, she'd hike as far as she could, just to be out there. And when walking was almost impossible, we'd find parking lot caches or caches in the desert where we could just about drive up to the cache. She would lean out the window and study the area, then direct us to the spot ... sure enough, it was always there! We would joke that if it wasn't where she pointed to, then it had to be missing!

In the six years that mom cached as BingoPat1, she found nearly 6,000 caches, hid dozens, cached in almost every state in the US, and in four different countries. And she brought countless people into the game with her wit and enthusiasm. We lost her in April of 2015, but were warmed with all the friends and family that came to celebrate her life. And as you might guess, the geocachers outnumbered everyone else; she'd have loved that!

# The First Day of Geocaching

Emily Stull
*Geostull*

I snuck around making sure not to be seen. People always talked about how you couldn't be seen while geocaching.

My family tried to look natural in the parking lot of Outback Steakhouse but we were struggling with our first cache. When we were finally ready to give up we noticed it... The bottom of the street light was not bolted down.

I tried not to run over to the lamp. Gotta look natural.

I was scared of lifting up the bottom of the lamppost because of bugs. Making sure no one was around, I quickly lifted up the bottom. I spotted the small canister almost immediately. I snatched it, and took it over to our car. My parents were amazed at how fast I had grabbed it and how sneakily I got it.

I was beaming.

First day, and I was already a pro!

Then again, it was only our first cache... My dad figured out how to sign the small roll of paper inside the small geocache. My dad handed me the canister and I rushed back to the lamppost. Again, I made sure no one was coming out of the restaurant. I quickly shoved the container back into the hiding spot, and ran back to our car.

We drove to our next cache which was in a Walgreen's parking lot. This was the most adventurous thing we'd done in ages!

I went straight for the light posts. Knowing the new knowledge of they weren't bolted down. I lifted up every one that was remotely close to our location. Nothing. I was confused. Wasn't the cache supposed to be under the metal box?

Then we decided to do something out of our geocaching comfort zones. Go near the road. We tried to walk as normally as we could to the road. Cars zoomed past, and we would check our shirts or brush off our jeans. We slowly made our way to the railing on the side of the road and started looking all around for a Ziplock container.

That's when my dad spotted a black thing on the railing. It was about the size of a playing card. They made geocaches that small? We were amazed and confused. How did we get it open? We took turns pulling and pushing what we thought was a lid. Then my dad had the brilliant idea of sliding.

It slid open easily and we all peaked inside the container.

The log was laid there just like any other cache.

My mom pulled it out, and signed out geocaching names. Geostull.

All that day, we drove around town, stopping at various parking lots. Finally we ran out of restaurant chains and convenience stores. We decided to be the most adventurous thing we've done all day.

Go into the woods.

We drove to a small wooded area that had a one-star terrain cache hidden there We were prepared. We had a secret weapon: bug spray!

We coated our legs with the substance. No bugs were getting on us today. We walked into the woods of six to ten trees. We looked around for a little bit. At last, I spotted a container wrapped in camouflage duct tape. My parents grabbed the log but my brother and I were way more interested into the small toys inside. My brother and I each grabbed a trinket we liked and remembered to leave something behind for the next geocacher.

When we got back to the car we checked each other for ticks. That wasn't so bad. We went to another cache that was nearby in a different small wooded area.

Slowly becoming geocaching pros, we immediately found the cache. My mom started picking out our next cache on the GPS when something fell on her arm. She looked down, and a snake slithered away.

Was that a snake?

Did it just touch my mother?

A snake touched my mother!

We ran back to the car!

You'd think that would be enough for a family who rarely gets out, but we couldn't quit now with so much daylight left!

I enjoyed the thrill of venturing off the paved path to find a prize. Apparently, so did the rest of my family. Then the most extraordinary thing popped up on our GPS: a trail with caches hidden along it.

The people who came up with this are amazing!

We rushed across town to the trail. We walked the trail finding caches as we went. And the bug spray worked; we only picking up a couple ticks! When we finally finished the trail, the summer sun was setting. Time to call it a day.

We went home satisfied with the day we had. When we went to bed that night little did we know how far we would come. Seeing a moose and her baby a little too close. Caching everyday for a year. Not even caring if a cache had a four star terrain. Finding a cache in five different states in one day.

It's stunning how far we have come from that first day.

# *Wonderland in Tucson*

Bruce Eldredge
*ESP Boss*

We were in Tucson, Arizona, to spend Thanksgiving with my in laws. (It's an annual family tradition.) After spending Black Friday making 40 dozen tamales (that's another family tradition) I needed to stretch my legs. Plus, a travel bug had been burning a hole in my pocket for weeks, and since the University of Arizona/Arizona State football game was no longer on Thanksgiving weekend, any excuse to get out of the small house was welcome! I decided to kidnap my wife and daughter to go after our first urban cache.

Living in rural Arizona, there just aren't that many caches that require super-stealthy skills to retrieve them without alerting the Muggles. And in the whole scheme of things, we were still new at the whole geocaching thing. (That's why I didn't see the hint on the cache page asking people not to drop travel bugs in this cache until the bug had already been left. Oops!)

This cache wasn't just urban; it was actually placed on private property. And what was even more surprising – the property owner wasn't the cache owner. In fact, we discovered on a trip back to that cache several months later, the property owner didn't even geocache. At all!

We pulled up to the curb and knew instantly that we were in the right place for a cache called Steel Menagerie (GCV6MP). Graceful metal flowers arched overhead – if flowers 15 feet tall and made from shovel heads can be called graceful. I felt as if I'd been transported to Wonderland – and simultaneously shrunk too. The GPS clearly showed that we were in the right place but with all these potential hiding places, getting to the actual location of GZ (and even finding the cache container) could be problematic.

As I worried about muggles, I looked over to see my wife and daughter slowly exploring, both of them wearing identical expressions of wonder. These weren't the "normal" metal sculptures of rocks surrounded with heavy-gage welded wire to make ants or spiders. Or the stereotypical metal sculptures of the southwest making javelina or barrel cacti.

This yard was full of the almost-familiar. Clearly humanoid figures but with surprising configurations and extra limbs. Creatures that couldn't be easily identified as mammal or insect; nothing was what was expected. It was fanciful, exciting, and almost eerie – but without being grotesque as so much "modern art" could be.

Pretty soon my daughter was lost behind her camera lens as she was getting up close and personal with the fantastical metal sculptures that surrounded us.

There was a "dragon" with six legs like an insect but clearly not a bug since it had fangs fashioned from old nails and a tail from some huge spring – as long as its body – and finished with a pointed shovel blade. Fanciful insects with rusted barbeque forks as feet and glass marbles somehow attached to the all-metal heads made from old car parts and rusted cans. Trumpet flowers arching higher than the roofline with rebar stamens and gently bobbing on springs-turned-stems.

As we wandered, somewhat afraid to venture off the path meandering though the yard to even look for the cache, a breeze stirred and hundreds of metal wind chimes clanked gently to life.

"I'll be the neighbors love that!" my wife exclaimed. Each chime might be soothing alone but en masse the effect was overwhelming.

My daughter was fixated on one sculpture – something like a rooster with the bristles from a steel brush as a comb and a huge, industrial gear for a head. Having learned how to weld in high school, and was carefully examining how the creatures and flowers had been put together. I could imagine the gears turning in her head about how to start collecting metal junk to create fanciful welded creations of her own.

I just hoped she moved out first…

As the November sun slanted westward, we remembered the reason for the trip: a geocache. I pulled the printed page from my pocket and re-read the hint: "What's for lunch?"

The GPS was focused on one area of the yard – an area that was crammed full of smaller creatures. I called to my family to see if we could actually focus enough to find the geocache – as fun as this was, I was very aware that we had spent nearly half an hour in someone else's front yard. I was worried about the neighbors – it was a holiday weekend after all so they might be on the lookout for suspicious activity if the homeowner wasn't there.

My daughter bravely stepped off the path and waded through the metal creations. She paused to consider a knee-high, dog like creature with too many legs. It vaguely resembled a dachshund. In its mouth, a small metal lunch box. She gently reached down to see if the clasp would open…

It did and inside was the log and the stub of the pencil. She fished it out and stepped back onto the path for us to sign and snap the requisite selfie. I slipped the travel bug back inside and we were on our way – back to the real life of a small house filled with family and laughter.

For our success, we went back to my in laws for tamales and left over pumpkin pie – yet another family tradition!

# The Ammo Can Find

Eunita Boatman
*Fairlady-Fisherman*

**First Time Number One:** In May 2008, I drove 92 miles to help a good friend – one I've been friends with for nearly 40 years - find a cache: a simple Difficulty 1.5, Terrain 1.5. I had introduced her to geocaching a few months prior, and she had spent the last three weeks looking for this particular cache without success, while other geocachers found it and logged it on the cache page. Each time she saw a new one, off she would rush to try her luck again. "I've been there 17 times; I'm just not seeing it," she whined.

Not overly excited about the drive, I took a day away from work, gassed up the jeep, and hit the road to Delhi, California, forgetting that I would also inevitably hit morning rush hour traffic in both Stockton and Modesto on my way. As fate would have it, I got a flat on the freeway in rush hour traffic. A nail in the tire was the culprit, and as I waited for AAA to show up, the traffic slowly dispersed.

For all intents and purposes, the rest of the trip to rural Delhi should have been quick. But then, a warning light on the dashboard came on, and I was tasked with finding a Jeep dealership, since the darn thing was still under warranty. After an hour's wait, it turned out to be nothing: the flat tire had signaled something else and it took all of 3 seconds for the mechanic to have me up and running again. (Note: by this time, I had four hours invested in a 95-minute trip, and I was still about 30 minutes away from Delhi.) First Time Number Two: getting a flat tire geocaching.

Finally, I arrived in Delhi. With the GPS loaded and paper printout in hand (yes, we still actually used paper back then!), we heaved the ice chest and goodie box into the Jeep and started the drive down the block, determined not to leave until we located this elusive cache. Less than a mile from her driveway, we had reached ground zero. Within minutes, I had spied the cache. But by this time, tired and dreading the trip back to Sacramento, I wanted to have a little fun, at someone else's expense. First Time Number Three: being a jerk!

I asked my friend (whose caching name is BunnyFun) to show me where she had already looked, and as we searched each location, I struck up a conversation about how the community of Delhi had not really grown a lot in the past 20 years or so. She agreed, and said that was why she loved the rural community. We searched in logical places: the exposed roots of orchard almonds, old farm equipment. BunnyFun told me she knew the owners, and they were aware of the cache as they had placed it themselves. This meant it was ok for us to explore.

We were, according to the paperwork, looking for an ammo box. It was a regular-sized cache, not a micro. However, BunnyFun had decided that it had to be a miniature ammo box, as there was no place for a regular size cache container of any size to be hidden at this location. First Time Number Four: having way too much fun at someone else's expense. I could have easily pointed out that we were looking for a regular-sized ammo box for sure.

After about half an hour of hearing "I looked there already" and "Not there either," I told my friend that I would recheck the coordinates, which were correct. Then, I stepped back and told her that the coordinates pointed to the road, in front of the rail fence. "Yes, but I checked the fence and there are no bushes. It's not there," she responded. "I even checked across the road, and it's not over there either."

I went back to asking her about Delhi, and the farms and agriculture of the area, and then I asked her when they got city water out there, since I had thought it was all well water. She answered, "We don't have city water out here; everyone is still on wells."

We were still at ground zero, mind you, and I was practically standing on a nice, well-placed cement water cover.

"Oh," I said.

She went on about looking at the fence again, checking each of the rails and all around the base of each post. First Time Number 5: trying to keep a straight face and not give away the location of a cache.

I simply remained standing right by the water cover, and sipped on a bottle of water, pretending I was checking the GPS. Then, when she finally walked back to me, defeat on her face, I dropped the water bottle on the cement water cover. That's when the light went on, and she realized why my questions about city water and wells were relevant. I only wish I were eloquent enough to describe the look on her face when she realized where the ammo box was located!

I let her do the honors of opening the lid of the water cover and removing the ammo box. Thankfully, the ammo can was filled with some very nice swag. She found her first path tag, and the smile on her face was almost (but not quite) worth the flat tire, driving all over Modesto looking for a Jeep dealership, and that miserable, traffic-filled drive back to Sacramento.

The moral of this story: value your friends, for sure, but have a little fun, as well!

Since that day in Delhi, we have traveled thousands of geocache miles together, even driving 500 miles out of our way to sign the "Mingo" log in Kansas on the way home from the Woodstock in Missouri. On that trip, we drove 5003 miles from California to Illinois, cached in eight states and logged over 200 caches!

# New Year's First to Find!

Charlie James
*Floobyfish*

"What do you want to do today?" I murmured.

"I don't know! The same thing we have done for the past nine days, I suppose."

It was New Year's Eve, 2015. I think both my boyfriend Mike and I had experienced just about enough of duvet days, films and chocolate. As much as we loved not being at work, doing the opposite and becoming two very lazy sloths had begun to take its toll on us.

"We could go shopping," I suggested. But he and I both knew we were pretty broke after Christmas, and that there was nothing we really needed or wanted.

"Maybe we should go walk the dogs. I feel like we haven't left this house in well over a week!" He was doing his best to persuade me, and even though I wanted to be out and about, the thought of walking our spaniels Tilly and Lucy around the block just didn't interest me.

"Mike, we are such a boring couple!"

"What's that supposed to mean?!" He looked at me, irritated.

I giggled slightly, realizing I must have hit a nerve with my choice of words.

"Oh I'm sorry! I just mean that we seem to be getting into a bad routine of lounging about all day long. It can't be good for us."

I knew very well that I had been stuck in a rut. It was becoming upsetting, even, that I didn't seem to have a purpose outside of work.

"Well ok! Let's go on an adventure then!" I looked at him like he had gone mad. What on earth was he talking about? The location we lived in couldn't even promise a thrilling walk, let alone a big day of adventure. Plus, it was late December, and it was FREEZING!

"Have you ever heard of Geocaching?" he asked me.

"Geo-what?" I said.

"Geocaching! I saw a video online a few months ago and it's where you use this app on your phone to find things hidden outdoors!" He seemed like he knew what he was talking about, but I still wasn't convinced.

"I don't understand? What do you mean 'hidden things'?"

"People go out and hide containers wherever they want, and then they publish it online for others to go find using coordinates."

He had my attention.

The thought of treasure hunting has always captured my interest, ever since I was young. My mum used to hide clues around the house that would lead to chocolate coins hidden in my sandpit in the garden. I loved it.

But then I remembered our location.

"Hang on a minute, there isn't going to be anything nearby in this little village. How far away do we have to go?" I knew this would be a catch.

"Well, according to the map there are ten within the town and the closest one is about a fifteen minute walk away!" He seemed pleased with his discovery. My excitement rushed back to me instantly; it was the coins in the sandpit, all over again.

"Prove it! Let me see!" I darted over to where he was sitting and landed quite abruptly next to him, trying to squirm my face in closer to his phone.

"Wow! Do those green dots show where they are all hidden?"

"Yep, do you fancy finding some?" He gloated.

"Let me get my boots on. I'll get Tilly and Lucy too! They could do with a walk!" He smiled and rolled his eyes in amusement as he watched me shuffling about with my coat and boots like an excited child.

Once we had everything we needed to find our first geocache, GC1ZPWC, (pen, some trinkets, our phones for direction, a sense of adventure and our two fluffy dogs) we were off! As we were walking, I wondered to myself why on earth I was getting so excited about going to a location that I have walked past a million times before. I knew the answer, of course. This time, there would be something there that most people had no idea existed!

"Right, this seems to be the area where is says it's hidden. Let's start looking!" Mike was shouting over the busy road traffic beyond the trees that hid us from the road.

I had no idea what I was looking for, let alone where to look! A garbage bag, a soggy cardboard box, a brick, a shoe … each item I picked up was with disappointment, knowing each was not the treasure I had been hoping for.

"Mike! What exactly are we looking for? This is really difficult!" We had been searching for at least twenty minutes and I was starting to get frustrated. He pushed his way through the large branches to stand next to me.

"I need to check my phone again, bear with me!" He shouted. I was grimacing, hopping from one foot to the other in impatience and in reaction to the freezing weather. Our two little dogs were looking up at us with eyes that seemed to say "Come on, you guys! It's boring just standing here!"

Mike finally saw what we had missed beforehand.

"Look! The hint says 'base of a tree' - that should narrow it down!"

"Okay then, you go that way and I'll go this way" We split up and searched every tree until I finally noticed something out of place.

A small rock the size of a fist was staring up at me, completely pristine compared to surrounding rocks nearby. It didn't look natural. It was too shiny. Dirtless.

I picked the unusual rock up and knew straight away I had the cache. It was light as a feather and felt like plastic!

"Mike!" I screamed! "I think I've got it!" I flipped it over, and there in great big bold letters, it read: GEOCACHE. I grinned with excitement; before I knew it Mike was by my side.

"Oh wow you really have got it!" I pulled at the plastic lid covering the bottom of the container and out popped a pristine logbook inside a small plastic bag.

"Ok so you need to sign both of our names on that logbook and also the date. Just write Mike and Charlie - 31/12/15."

I unraveled the paper and took out my pen with freezing blue hands. I wrote in tiny letters both of our names and the date.

"There we go! Do you want to put it back since I found it?"

"Yeah, give it here." Mike rolled the paper back up and placed it back inside the rock cache.

We climbed back up to the main footpath feeling accomplished and excited about finding our first cache. This was what I had been waiting for! A sense of adventure and anticipation! It seemed so simple, geocaching. All you're doing is finding containers that other people have left intentionally for you! The world's largest treasure hunt!

"Mike, this could be a really great hobby for us. When you look at the map, there are caches hidden in every corner of the world!" I adopted a Cheshire cat grin in the hopes that we could go look for more, right then.

"I know! We can go whenever you'd like!" He looked up at the sky as he spoke, and then quickly back to me. The sky was starting to turn grey and blustery.

"I think it's going to rain, we should get back home." I looked down at my two little dogs who I knew would be displeased if they were to get too soggy, and said "Ok - let's do this again tomorrow and find as many as we can!" We smiled, and with that, rushed through the trees to get home as the first drop of rain landed on my nose.

# Snowy Southern California FTF

Kelly Rysten
*Rysten*


Almost all cities in America have what we call an
FTF Hound. My city is no different. Our most famous FTF
hound is w01f. Locals almost don't stand a chance against him.
He finds caches in the dead of night without a flashlight. The
only way to get an FTF where I live is to do it while w01f is out
of town. We have managed to get a few FTFs in our
geocaching lifetime but those times were either caches that
w01f placed himself or were part of a series and we met him in
the middle. He was always a good sport and seemed to enjoy
meeting other geocachers on the geotrail. We compared notes
so we would know which caches where still FTF possibilities.
So when a series of caches published and there was no FTF all
day we began to speculate. Was w01f out of town? Was he
sick? The next day there were still no FTFs logged. At this
point I became curious enough to read further.

I am not an FTF hound. Sure, an FTF would be cool. We
didn't even have one yet, but surely we would get there and
find all the logs signed. It was pointless to venture out just to
check. The day wore on. I watched the cache pages. No logs

were posted. Finally, the day became boring and TSPI and I wanted to get out. Why not drive up to see where those new caches were? We had never been there before. How hard could it be? Then we thought that if w01f hadn't found them they might be impossible to get to. W01f had a Jeep. He could go anywhere we could. Still, there was only one way to find out and we wanted to get out of the house anyway, so off we went.

Let me just say that perhaps if a cache isn't FTFed in a timely manner there might be a reason. We could see on the map that the caches were on a mountain top between Los Angeles and Palmdale, California. There is a long mountain range the separates the Antelope Valley from the LA Basin. This was one of the minor mountains overlooking a valley and the highway that connects the two. The valley was filled with large houses built on horse property. The roads were mostly paved until we drew close to the mountain. Our GPS led us to a small road and we could see it off in the distance slanting up the mountain. However, between us and the mountain were the houses and every driveway looked precisely like a dirt road with Private Property signs. They were everywhere.

We studied our GPS screens trying to decide which were driveways and which were public roads. Then we studied the signs wondering which were only there to dissuade the gullible and which signified shot gun wielding ranchers.

Dogs ran beside our SUV barking warnings and greetings with equal enthusiasm. Horses watched as we drove slowly past their corrals. Usually, they only saw their owners and neighbors on this road. Who were these strange people?

Finally, we reached the bottom of the hill and a washed out dirt road led up the hillside. Our Explorer bumped and lurched its way to the top. It didn't take long for us to have a great view over all the small ranches below. We stopped and found a few caches on the way up since nobody else seemed to be out and about that day. The wind howled and we shivered through every search.

When we reached the top of the mountain we could see three valleys below us. Through the snow. The sky above was blue, but the snow was blowing across the mountain at us sideways.

Finding our target cache involved searching a rock outcropping on top of the mountain. The wind whistled around us, threatening to blow us off. These southern California residents love snow, though we prefer to see it from the comfort of home. Being blown off a snowy mountain wasn't part of the plan.

There are a lot of rock hides in the desert. Sometimes they are easy and sometimes they are difficult. They can be mind-numbingly tedious. This hunt fell square in the middle of all of those. The cache turned out to be a camouflaged tube hidden in a crevasse with a rock over it to hide it from the casual observer. We sat on top of the outcropping, my hair blowing in front of my face. We opened the cache and pulled out the log sheet. It was in a little jewelry bag so we opened the bag with numb fingers. I carefully unfolded the log sheet as it whipped around in the wind. We were first! FTF! We traded for a black Hot Wheels car so we would have a souvenir of our first First to Find. Then we found the next cache, which was also an FTF, but we decided to leave the rest of the trail for someone else. We achieved our goal. The first few FTFs were ours. The rest of them we left for somebody else to enjoy. We had a challenging drive, some miserable weather, a not too challenging search for the cache and a grand view. We were glad we ventured out of the house that day. I bet the next geocachers up the hill had a little less adventure, but they logged many more FTFs than we did.

# Was that Peanut Butter Jar Worth it?

Freddie Crusoe
*cruiser5*

After being cooped up inside more days than we cared to admit during the winter of 2014, my geocaching friend Jenni (Hokum124) and I decided to spend a lovely spring day geocaching. We headed out about 45 minutes from my house and spent the day finding a variety of caches. That afternoon, we came upon a park that contained several geocaches. We crossed over a bridge, over the prairie trail, and then off into the woods.

The mud on the trail was nearly an inch deep, but that didn't stop us. The first cache was about 300 feet away across a swampy area; we decided not to try for that one as it was early April and the water would be pretty cold. There is always another cache, right?

So off we went for the next cache. This time our road block wasn't a swamp, but a river. The river was high due to all the melted snow and I told Jenni,

"There has to be a way across this river, let's keep looking."

We moved further down the river bank. We couldn't find any shallow places to cross and then suddenly there it was! Just what we were looking for! A tree bent over the river and shaped like a rainbow. I looked at Jenni and said "Rainbows lead you to treasures!" Or in this case, a geocache.

I climbed up and onto my rainbow shaped bridge and shimmied my way across. Reaching the other side, getting down wasn't a problem. But I knew coming back might be… But, heck, you always worry about that after you sign the log, right?

Crossing the muddy ground, I made my way to ground zero, searching for the elusive cache. There was no way I wanted to leave with a DNF. I finally spied it way up on top of a narrow tree. Oh my, how was I going to get that down?

Turns out it was easier than I thought! Then I was off onto the return trip to find Jenni who was waiting for me on the other side of the rainbow bridge.

Once I reached the tree, I was proud that I could maneuver my vertically-challenged body up and onto the bent tree so I could complete the return trip. Jenni was recording my adventure on her cell phone. She commented out loud, "It would be really funny if you fell."

I replied, "No it wouldn't and don't jinx me!"

Then I continued across the tree, nearing the far side. Jenni stopped recording because her phone battery was almost dead. Reaching the section of the tree that curved down, I decided I needed to turn over onto my belly so I could shimmy down the tree.

Moving my right foot up onto the log I prepared to turn. OH NO! My foot slipped! I scrambled desperately to find something to grab onto, the small branches were no match for my falling body… Boom! I slammed onto the ground. My right ankle took the brunt of my weight and then twisted sideways into the mud.

Jenni wanted to laugh but was afraid I was hurt. I lifted myself up, cursing like a sailor! I started to laugh so I wouldn't cry and Jenni burst into laughter. She wasn't laughing at me but with me. I tried to stand and couldn't get up; Jenni offered to carry me on her back. I had her find me a Y-shaped tree branch that I could use as a crutch and then had her help me walk out. It was 3 blocks to the car through the mud, each step taken cautiously. Once we reached my vehicle, I asked Jenni to drive me home.

My husband (The Muggle) watched as we pulled into the yard, noticing that Jenni was driving. I called him over and he shook his head no. Eventually walking over to the car and asking "What happened?" Explaining the story to him, he just shook his head and said,

"Was that peanut butter jar worth it?"

Of course my answer was yes.

I rested up that night and went to the doctor the next morning, believing all along that I only had a sprained ankle. Sadly, it was broken. When the doctor asked what happened, I had to explain geocaching. They sent me to a specialist and he cast my leg. Jenni went to several of my appointments with me. Each time someone would ask "What happened?" I would look at Jenni and say, "She pushed me out of a tree!"

We would laugh and then explain geocaching. Once again each time someone would ask, "Was that peanut butter jar worth it?"

And always my answer would be "Yes!"

By the way, we did learn after the fact that we entered the park from the backside. Had we gone in from the other side, we would never have had to cross the river! Just goes to show a geocacher will make any caching trip an adventure!

# 5/5: Caching The Sacadaga

Daniel Rhodes Jr
*Lord Scoville*

"Want me to see if I can find out if the boulders are in place at the 100th cache? I am off this week and could go with you if you are up for it?" This is the message sent to me by cdparker1.

A few short days later it would lead to my first 5/5 cache and to an experience that would change my life forever. After determining that the boulders (used to block access to the road during the winter months) were not yet in place, we made plans to grab breakfast, then trek out to GC14T9M "CDPARKER's 100TH CACHE."

At approximately 9:00am on October 23, 2015, I met cdparker1 at the Northampton Diner on Route 30 in Northampton, New York. We ordered our breakfasts, he had a ham and cheese omelet with wheat toast and home fries, and I enjoyed a western style omelet with bacon, wheat toast, and a hot coffee. The food was phenomenal, the atmosphere was warm and welcoming, and prices were decent. Over breakfast, we discussed our previous caching experiences and goals for future caching expeditions. After breakfast we hopped in my van and made our way to the trailhead located at White House in Wells, New York.

I'm always amazed by the beauty of the Adirondacks. The trip from the diner to the trailhead took us alongside the Sacandaga River, a 64 mile long river that twists and turns through the Adirondack State Park from Lake Pleasant to the Hudson River. The red, yellow, and orange colors of fall highlighted our journey and set the mood for the adventure ahead.

When we arrived at the trailhead, we donned our safety gear (it was hunting season after all), grabbed our hiking sticks, and ventured into the woods. The main trail was well marked with trail markers, but that didn't help us much. Of the three or four miles in to the cache, a cacher is only going to follow the main trail for a quarter of a mile. With fallen leaves blanketing the forest floor and nothing marking the side trail, we nearly missed our first turn.

"It's your cache," I joked, "shouldn't you know where the trails turn off?" That cocky attitude would later bite me in the butt. We followed the side trail in about a mile and a half to where it crossed the river. We made a pit stop, he performed maintenance on a friend's cache that was nearby, then we continued on.

I remembered this section from a previous attempt at this cache so I brought along a change of shoes and socks in the event that I had to tread water. The water was low at this time of year which made rock hopping a viable option. I took it slow, using my hiking stick to keep me upright and on the rocks. My right foot had other plans. I stepped on a rock that was obviously slippery and firmly planted my foot and half of my leg in the very cold water.

"How's the water?" I heard from behind me.

"Effing cold. How do you think it is," I replied. I figured I was already wet so I'd just walk through the water to the other side. I turned to watch cdparker1 cross flawlessly.

"Showoff," I said.

He laughed, but was kind enough to wait for me to change my socks and shoes, after which we continued on our way.

Now that we had crossed the river, what had once been a very obvious trail was now little more than a bushwhack. Still the terrain was doable and we continued on. At about two miles from the cache we came across a set of mini waterfalls rushing from between two boulders. It was here that I decided to place a cache of my own titled "Mini Falls" GC65KFK.

After placing the cache we took our first real water break and took in the views. The colors of the changing leaves, the shining of the late morning sun, and the stillness of the river painted a picture of a serene environment that is reminiscent of a Gainsborough painting. We gathered our packs and continued onward.

At about one third of a mile from our destination the trail continued to thin until it simply disappeared. A deer trail continued up and over a rocky cliff, but our path was to continue skirting the river. I stopped and said, "It was from up there that I fell last time while attempting to get down here." He laughed and said that he had had a similar mishap in or around this area.

We had traveled only a few hundred feet when we came to a section where there was no other option but to hug the cliff and feel for rocks to use as a path. The problem that had presented itself was not in hugging the cliff nor in finding sturdy rocks, but in getting safely to this path. When looking for the best way to approach this challenge, we found what we thought was the best option. It wasn't until we were too far in that we realized that another option had been available and that we had missed it.

We were probably five feet above where we needed to be, but the rock on which we were standing didn't allow us to simply step or scoot down. If we had tried, we would have stepped into fast-moving water and probably killed ourselves. The best option from here was to cling to a root that was jutting out just over where we needed to be; cdparker1 made this look easy. He grabbed hold of the root, and safely lowered himself to the thin, rocky path beneath.

Now it was my turn.

I grabbed that root like a bear clinging to a branch in its

attempt retrieve honey from a hive. Like a bear I clung firmly, but because I could not see the rocks beneath me, I froze. My fear of heights kicked in and all I could think was that I was going to fall and kill myself.

In the middle of laughing at me cdparker1 said, "Put your foot back here."

"Where? I can't see a damn thing," I said. My heart was pounding and my adrenaline was pumping.

"Move your left foot back and set it down on the rock."

"What rock? I don't see a rock."

"Just do what I said." By now he was nearly on ground from laughing so hard.

I attempted to place my foot on the rock that I couldn't see. "Where the f—k is this damn rock?" He grabbed my foot and set it on the rock. Once I had my footing I was fine and able to lower myself. I let out a scream of success and said, "Now that was an adrenaline rush." I quickly regained my composure and onward we went.

After skirting the river for a few hundred yards we were back on dry, stable land. The trail was completely gone and the remainder of the hike would be a bushwhack. We continued on without incident until we were about 300' from the cache. It's also 300' from the cache that the terrain changes drastically. There is no soft ground to walk, only large boulders to climb, alongside a beautiful set of waterfalls. Needless to say, I was a bit nervous, because a fall from these rocks could prove fatal. More than being nervous, I was in awe of the scenery before me. A few pictures to take home with me and a brief rest, then it was on to locate the cache. My GPS was jumpy, but once it settled I made the find fairly quickly.

After I made the find, we ate lunch on the boulders and reflected on our adventure. We relaxed for about ten to fifteen minutes, then began our trek back to the van. Shortly after starting our return trip, I lost my footing and down I went on my knees. The three or four miles back were painful, but free of any mishaps. We got back to the van a little after four that evening, stopped to grab two more caches, then back to the diner to grab his car.

This cache and the adventure that went along with it goes down as my most memorable and favorite cache to date. I claimed it changed my life and it has. I faced my fear, proved to myself that I am strong and maybe a little crazy, and I gained a true friend in a fellow geocacher.

# *A Challenge Cache First to Find*

Laura Ready
*Wa wa*


Going on a FTF run is like reaching into the great unknown. Even more difficult is going for a FTF on a challenge cache, as you not only have to find the cache, but you also have to figure out how to get your hands on the log. So here's the tale of my first attempt at a challenge cache using a battery on a geocache called Home Tweet Home GC5WET2. It's a story of (mis) adventure, to say the least!

I had heard whispers that there were techie challenges being set up by the CO of this one, and was waiting with excitement to see what marvelous creations or adaptations were in store for us with the fantastic series at Annacrivey Woods. I hadn't seen this notification come in the previous night, and when it was still unfound that morning, I decided on a whim to go for it. I have never gone to a cache before armed with a PP3 battery. It all seemed very interesting. In all honesty, I was also a bit concerned that I might not know what to do once I got there. I was frankly worried I'd end up electrocuting myself, as I'm fairly accident prone.

There were no surprises then that it turned out to be a bit of a saga - all of my own making. I did try to prepare properly... I swear! I had the battery at the ready (I promise I did not take one out of the smoke alarms). I came in from a FTF run on the Royal Canal, and changed into the hiking boots, grabbed a banana for breckie along with the battery, and set off from the suburbs of Dublin for Enniskerry.

Parking was an issue and time is money on a FTF run, so I tried to get as close as I could to the cache. I ventured up a steep narrow road with barely enough room for a car in an attempt to save hiking time in the woods. This road could only be described as a "road" in the loosest of terminology, as it was filled with pot holes and had grass growing up through the middle of it. I found a tiny corner of level ground adjacent to a ditch, and hauled the car in off the road as far I could get it without toppling it into the ditch. I hoped there was enough room for a tractor to pass.

I ran up the steep trail and into the wood. It was early morning, all was quiet apart from the birdsong, my breathing, the sound of my feet crunching on the gravelly path and my heart thumping from the exertion. I took in great gulps of the lovely fresh countryside air, and tried to calm my nerves as I'm always a bit nervous heading into woods alone.

Then I managed to do a series of silly things that doubled the challenge factor. When I was just at GZ, I put by hand in my pocket and realised the battery was in the back seat in the car. Back down the steep hill I went, puffing louder than Thomas the Tank engine, and back up again.

I climbed over a ditch and headed into the forest, stepping over mossy ground and fallen logs, and soon saw the marvellous contraption. What a lovely surprise! It was a bird house placed high on a trunk of a tree.

Now, what to do with this? Would I be tall enough to reach it? Nope. Half way was as far as I could get. So I looked around for something to stand on, found an old bokedy, wonky plastic oil drum in a nearby field, and dragged it over to balance precariously on top of it.

I reached up and tried a few things that made sense if you're trying to get a battery to work. Zilch. I stood looking at it.

Maybe it's voice-activated I thought, so I sang it a Coronas song. Nothing. I was glad there was no else around. There I was early morning in the depths of a forest, singing to a wooden box.

Movement activated then? I shook a stick at it. Still nothing. I was stumped. "Perhaps there is something on top that I am missing," I thought. But I couldn't reach. I stretched more, fell off the oil drum and climbed back on again. Hmmmm. I finger searched everywhere, no joy. By this stage, I was praying someone else would come to join in the search! It marked about the only time that I was on a First to Find run that I actually hoped to see another geocacher. The woods were quiet. No sign of anyone. Hmmmm.

I thought about ringing the hubbie who was still in the cot and was having a Saturday lie on. I imagined his response would have been a 7-letter word starting in D and ending in E. (When I asked later if he would have been a willing PAF, he said my imagined word choice was wrong, and there would have been two words not one: the first starting with and the second ending with a letter 2 spaces further on in the alphabet.) I was baffled. I sat on the oil drum, ate my banana, and tried to reason it out. I googled the size of the battery. It looked fine. Then the thought suddenly came to me: what if the battery was dead? GAAAA!!!!

So off I went again down the hill. I didn't have another in my box of tricks in the car, so I left my "parking" spot (all the while praying it would be still there when I got back and not occupied by another geocacher's car as that would mean a far longer hike) and drove back down the narrow potholed road and a couple of kilometers away to the nearest village called Enniskerry.

The village was still half asleep, with only a few shops open. I raced into the Spar where the shopkeeper was writing down a list of purchases on tick for a customer in the most beautiful cursive script (didn't know they did that anymore). I thought "HURRY UP!" while I hopped impatiently from one leg to the other.

Finally! The battery cost an extortionate 6.99, but there was no time for debate. I set off again. My "parking" space was empty. Happy days! I climbed the hill yet again … still puffing.

Now the cache itself is a marvelous gadget, once you come with the right equipment, and it worked immediately! A few little sparks could be seen and a clicking noise heard. OPEN SESAME! Wahooo. There it was - a lovely blank log.

The CO Yer Man certainly devised a wonderful cache and challenge factor. It must have taken a very long time to set up. I had never seen this type of cache before. I was delighted with the FTF prize of a flash light. It was especially apt as I could do with a few more light bulbs, especially in the brain department! I made sure to keep the fully charged battery in a safe place in case it would be needed again.

It certainly was an adventure that I will never forget! It's not every day you start off in the depths of the woods at an ungodly hour in the morning while the rest of the world sleeps looking for a geocache with a flat battery. I got some teasing after it, let me tell you!

# We Did See the Sign...

Maggie Fisher
*shrimala*

For the record, we *did* see the "Primitive Road" sign.

To understand my story, you have to know a few things. In Eastern Washington, spring can get muddy. And when I say "muddy," I mean squelching, slippery, nasty mud that can be six or more inches deep, and you can sink right down into it without even knowing what happened. The roads between wheat fields are usually well-marked with big, friendly warning signs that say "primitive road." But of course we usually blow right past them, as we almost never go out caching in remote areas in anything but summer and fall.

This spring, my fiancé Derek and I had the opportunity to go to a GeoEvent in the abandoned ghost town Elberton, Washington. I remembered the town: its beautiful, still-standing church from the 1800s, the little houses and old farm equipment with grass overgrown in the yard. I also remembered the rough gravel roads leading to town, and thought Derek's crimson Pontiac Vibe, *The Coug Mobile*, might handle them better.

We loaded our car with granola bars and fellow cachers and off we went. The day was grey and drippy, but the heavy rains promised by the news anchors were not making an appearance. We wandered the town, found a few caches, snapped some photos, and headed out for the next closest cache.

Normally when caching, I play the role of navigator. I pre-check the routes, make sure we are going to be on good roads, and then stare at my smartphone maps and compare against Nüvi, as I often disagree with her driving directions. On this day, as we had other cachers in the car, I was in the back seat and therefore ignoring Nüvi. I looked around, enjoying the scenery and chatting as we headed toward the cache, and we ended up in Garfield, Washington.

Wait, what?

Why were we in Garfield, I wondered. The cache was at least 5 miles behind us at that point!

"I highly disagree with Nüvi. We should turn around and try again from Elberton. It would be faster," I said.

No one disagreed, so off we went on our merry little way to try again. We got almost back to Elberton, then turned on the 'faster' route that I had found.

Again, we *did* see the sign. Primitive Road.

We just ignored it.

We didn't really think about the recent rains, and the mud it had caused. As we went slipping and sliding along the road, it was clear that this was not the best navigation decision I had ever made. It was also clear that The Coug Mobile was simply not cut out for mud, or rain, or primitive roads in the spring storms of Eastern Washington.

So there we were, slipping and sliding all over the road, narrowly missing ditches several times. This did nothing to help the high anxiety I have about cars, and despite my trust in my fiancé's driving, it was clear that the car was out of control. It was like we were on black ice!

The stress was palpable between us; we were all tense. I was hanging from the grab bar above my head, desperately trying to make it through the Lord's Prayer, and hoping that it would count as asking for help. No, apparently, it was not going to help us on our terrifying slip and slide journey to ground zero.

When we finally squelched to a halt, we were nearly a mile

from the end and our car had slipped sideways, finally resting against a high bank on the passenger side. As I stared numbly at the branches scratching the side of the car, I realized something.

*I'd never gotten stuck when geocaching. I had no idea what to do!*

Derek hopped out of the car and looked around. He checked the tires, shook his head at the mud, and then announced that we were not going forward, but turning around and going back instead.

Back on the slippery, muddy, worse-than-black-ice road, which we had just nearly died to get two miles down. We knew that pavement was a mere mile out of reach, if only we could get the car to go forward.

With some fancy driving by Derek, who miraculously kept us from sliding into the ditch, we got the car turned around and started back the way we came. With high hopes, we made it a whole mile before the car got stuck again. At this point, we wondered if the car could get unstuck on its own minus three passengers.

Of course, the clouds and wind picked this exact moment to let loose on us. Knowing it was going to be wet and miserable out of the lovely heat of the car, I grabbed my umbrella and jacket, and joined my friends out in the wind and rain to cheerlead from the sidelines. We were all trying to not just blow away, in the mayhem.

As soon as we were out and Derek attempted to get the car moving again, we saw what was happening, and our hearts sank right into that six inch mud.

*The Coug Mobile had front-wheel drive!*

It's nearly *impossible* to navigate in slippery, gross mud with a front-wheel drive car.

So, for the first time in all of my geocaching adventures, I found myself behind a car and pushing. I was horribly embarrassed that my navigational error put us in this situation, and that my friends were outside pushing in the deep mud and torrential rain alongside me.

As we pushed and squelched inch-by-inch behind the car in the mud, I couldn't help but hope that the car wouldn't take off so quickly that we would all squelch face first into the mud, like some horrible cartoon, and stand up like a mud monster from the bog, half drowned in the rain!

Thankfully, with our pushing, the car made it off the primitive road. As we crawled back into the warm insides of *The Coug Mobile*, wet, cold and shivering, muddy to our knees, the weather seemed to sense we were inside again, and the sun came out.

Once again, we ended up in Garfield. As we pulled out of town headed home in cold defeat, *one of our party found a paved road to that very same cache.*

We went to the cache, excited to finally get to ground zero, and quickly made the find.

All that ... for a 35mm film canister under a rock.

We were wet, muddy, cold and miserable, but it was absolutely worth it.

# Burnin' Gas!

Mike Henderson
*SMTroop90*

Somehow, I managed to convince my wife to
venture out with myself and my usual caching companions,
Cara the Irish Wolfhound and Bear the Black Lab in my 40-
year old Jeep across part of Alabama and into rural Mississippi
on a backwoods caching excursion with some friends. She,
although not a cacher, was game that day, so with a
backpacking lunch stowed, an extra can of gas strapped on the
back bumper, and a bit of day hiking gear, we were off to the
Magnolia State.

We navigated our way through the woods along logging
roads, bouncing and jostling in the cramped old Jeep; my wife
was not impressed. At what seemed like a rather random place,
we found the GZ for the event, which was a cacher picnic
gathering in the woods. The dogs bailed out to explore the
kaleidoscope of newfound olfactory pleasures just waiting to be
inhaled, while we set up our stoves to prepare our feast of roast
beef, mashed potatoes and English peas. After lunch, our
woodland wanderings began, in the company of two exuberant
canines and a dozen or so caching friends. My observation

skills have since come under my own questioning, as I failed to heed the significance of the extra bag of gear being carried on our trek by one of the other cachers: the beginning of a future "Duh huh" moment.

Throughout the afternoon, several celebratory "hootie" yells echoed through the Mississippi woods when finds were made and ink was blotted on logs - that is, until we came upon "Burnin Gas!" Why it had such a name I cannot fathom. The CO who was with us sported a mischievous grin, and with a smooth extension of his index finger, he pointed. Up in the far reaches of a not-so-large tree was the container; easy to see, but certainly out of reach.

My first "Duh-huh" moment of the day happened as the zipper on the gear bag was pulled and the ropes, harness, and a plethora of climbing gear was spread on the ground. "Duh-huh" moment two was the realization that each one of the cachers present were experienced tree climbers, except one, and that one was me. "Duh huh" moment number three was not allowing common sense to prevail. Instead, I volunteered to climb the tree with bravado to spare and the swagger of a flamboyant pirate.

I had never climbed a tree before; this was to be my first. Well, as a kid, maybe I did ... as in a few feet high into the lower limbs of a backyard willow. But I had never climbed anything using the things my caching companions called ascenders, screwlock carabiners, descenders and power cams. That third "Duh-huh" moment became more worrisome as I realized I should have kept my mouth shut and hidden in the foliage, waiting for someone else to don gear. With ego pushing aside common sense, I was rigged up.

Allow me to state now that there is blotted ink on the log, albeit a rather squiggly "TL" for "Team Lunch" as it was done with by my trembling, sweaty hand. I signed it with witnesses, although they may have been wiping tears of laughter from their eyes or rolling on the ground by that time, holding their aching sides. I was so glad to have been the source of their entertainment for such an extended period of time; I swear, I think the dogs were even laughing.

I normally didn't do that type of thing. I am comfortable with my feet firmly planted on terra firma. The witnesses can verify that I displayed a complete lack of understanding and ability to accomplish what I was supposed to be doing.

The cache owner's name, "Team Xtreme" was appropriate, because that person was the reason several ugly words were muttered that day, and while I was uttering those words, he responded with gleeful laughter. On one of the tree limbs, a limb with a comparable diameter of a #2 pencil, was the cache. And there I stood, my prominent girth straining the climbing harness, which had, by the way, been loosened up to the last available strap holes to accommodate my torso. The CO gave me what might have been a detailed and useful set of instructions on how to use the gear, but I simply don't recall any of it as the panic was setting in, my focus entirely upon the ropes connecting me to the tree top.

It was time to climb. "Yea, I can do this," a statement that felt very similar to the classic "Here, hold my beer and watch this," which in my case should be reworded as "Lord, when the classic words 'Here, hold my beer and watch this' are uttered with me present, please oh please let me be the one holding two beers instead of one."

Today, someone else held my beer.

Things started out badly; I nearly kicked both CotonTop3 and Giber54 while struggling a mere two feet off the ground. Then things got worse, as the rope supporting my now suspended overweight mass managed to bring down two large limbs, one nearly hitting Giber54 and the other getting CotonTop3 on the bridge of his nose. Personally, little sympathy was shared, as they were beginning to giggle at my ineptness. From what I understand of how this was supposed to work, my being was supposed to be vertical: that is my feet at the lowest point and my head at the highest point. But for some strange reason, I think due to the gravitational pull on my robust upper torso, I somehow became horizontal, and maybe even a little inverted. Simple Cliff Note version: my gut weighs far more than my legs and feet, and once in this prone position I could not regain the desired upright posture. Things were really getting ugly.

My wife, who suddenly became an expert in the strengths of materials as related to timber structures, pointed out that the tree trunk that was supporting my weight was far too weak and was already splitting. More ugly words directed at the CO from me, as I continued to hear chuckles from below as well as my wife's detailed analysis of the deteriorating condition of the tree trunk (so much for spousal support and encouragement). As for the instruction and encouraging support of the other folks watching, I think they simply gave up. Instead, as I dangled, I heard their giggles, chuckles and guffaws, while trying to politely hold in their howls of laughter. Suffice it to say, they were not successful.

I dangled, I swung, I struggled. I grunted and cursed and farted. I dropped my hat which Bear the Lab retrieved. "Slide the gold one up the rope" was a frequent shout from below that was uttered between bouts of laughter. "Use your leg, stand up and push yourself up." Hey, that was not going to happen: overcoming the gravitational pull was far beyond my ability. Oh what fun on a Saturday afternoon in Mississippi!

I heard a joke once about having a heart attack: "The worst place to have a heart attack is during a game of charades." Not so, my friend, not so. I have found the worst place, and that would be dangling on a rope from a small tree in the woods in rural Mississippi with your best caching friends and your spouse groveling with laughter below. No compassion was shared for me.

After what seemed an hour of misery, my fingerprints were placed on the container and I managed to scrawl the initials "TL" on the log then crammed it back into the container. I dropped the pen to the ground and released the descender for a rapid ride back to terra ferma. I crash landed on my back on the ground, and the only consoling I received came from Bear the Black Lab who came over and laid his head on my heaving chest. Good dog, he even brought back my hat. Everyone else was propped against trees, laughing and wiping tears. I laid there with Bear, trying to still my pounding heart.

I got to hear my wife's rendition on the way home to

Alabama. At times, I could not understand what she was saying as she kept choking up with laughter. It must have been quite the show. As the CO noted in his log, it was an "adventure."

I am glad I managed contribute to the day by making the grab, and now I too can laugh at my rather unorthodox manner of ascending a tree in the Mississippi woods: my first tree climb.

Good times particularly after returning to earth. I am glad I got to do it, and glad my friends enjoyed as well.

# Midnight Multi-Cache

Molly Houser
*GeopenguinsH*

The story of the first midnight cache the
GeopenguinsH found began in the bathroom. One afternoon, I
was straightening my unruly hair (which I hate doing) but since
I was going to a friend's house that evening, I figured I needed
to look respectable. While working on this grueling task, my
friend from the 5swans5 called me. I answered the phone and
put her on speaker, hoping she could entertain me through my
self-induced torture.

She wanted to know where I was and what I was doing. I
told her I was doing my hair and she didn't believe me. I
insisted that is what I was doing. She was well-aware of how
long it takes me to tame my hair into submission. She asked if I
was really in my bathroom, or on my way to get the new multi-
cache. My response was "What new multi-cache?!" I had not
received any email notification for a new multi-cache.

I checked my email, and nothing! I checked the geocaching
app, and there it was! It was a new multi-cache called "Eliza
Jane Thomas" (GC473D5). It was 4 stages beginning at a
nearby cemetery. I was furious! Being a "First to Find" hound,

I typically drop everything to go after a new cache. My friend told me she was at the first stage and I knew there was no way I could get the FTF before her. I continued to angrily straighten my stupid hair while thoughts of just shaving it off flooded my mind. I stayed on the phone with her while she grabbed the coordinates at the second stage and arrived at the third. She had difficulty finding the container at the third stage, and ended up leaving. There was at least one other geocacher looking for the stages, so I figured it was pointless to run out and grab it even though she had left without the final coordinates.

I left to go to my friend's house and the first stage happened to be at a large cemetery that was on the way. I figured I might as well stop at the first stage and grab the coordinates for the second stage. After getting the coordinates, I checked the time and decided the second stage was not that far away. I arrived at another cemetery which was smaller than the first and quickly found the coordinates for the third. Looking at my watch again, I pondered whether I wanted to be on time for my friend's event, or get the coordinates for the third stage. "What good is being on time really?" I asked myself. That's no fun. I went after the third stage. The third stage was at a cemetery smaller than the previous two. I had as much trouble finding the coordinates for the final stage as my friend did. There was nothing in the place where the hint suggested it might be. I was there awhile losing track of time, getting muddy and dirty. Finally, it was too dark to see and I abandoned my search and headed to my friend's house.

While there, all I could think about was getting the final coordinates. Where could they be? I kept sneaking my phone out and refreshing the app to see if anyone had found it. No one had logged it! My friend had not gone back for it and the other cacher had not found it. I also finally received the "new cache" notification email for the multi-cache. There must have been some glitch and my notification was finally sent out ... not that it did me any good then.

Once my friends event was over, I sent my husband a text and let him know that I was coming home to get our oldest son and some light sources as it was then dark and late in the evening. He was not interested in joining us, as he is not a fan of traipsing around cemeteries in the middle of the night.

I picked up my oldest son and we headed back to the third stage. I am sure that we checked every single nook and cranny in the tiny cemetery. The container with the final coordinates was nowhere to be found. We looked around for over an hour in the chilly night air. My frustration increased with each degree that the temperature dropped.

I knew the name of the multi-cache had to be important. There were no graves with that name at the third cemetery. I did a grave locater search on my phone for Eliza Jane Thomas in Pulaski county Missouri and hit the jackpot. I read about a single lonely grave in the middle of the Mark Twain National Forest. It was often referred to as a "witch's grave" by the locals. There were 2 different pages with 2 different descriptions on how to get there. Even thought I had no final coordinates, I figured it was worth a shot. I asked my son if he was tired and wanted to go home. He said that he did. I told him this was not the time to give up and we followed the first set of directions.

The first set of directions led us down a paved road past a rock quarry several miles from the third cemetery. We ended up in a neighborhood that did not seem right. We should have been in the woods. My geosense told me that we were not in the right place, so we turned around.

The second set of directions involved us getting on the freeway and heading several miles east. After that we followed a highway several miles south and turned onto a dirt Forest Service Road. Spooky is not a powerful enough word to describe the road that we had turned onto. It was dark and thick with pine trees on both sides. There was a huge hole full of muddy water across the road that we drove through. The road was marked with many other potholes, rocks and logs. I knew we were on the correct road.

As I drove down the creepy road I wondered how big this grave really was. People said it was right there and you couldn't' miss it, but I was worried that we would pass it somehow since it was so dark out. So far, the description of the road and directions were spot on.

We reached a point in the road where we needed to turn. I made a left turn as indicated in the directions and continued on. A few hundred feet after the turn I saw it: there was no missing it even in the pitch dark. Rocks were piled up to make a grave measuring about 3 feet high, 6 feet wide and 10 feet long. There was a wooden placard nailed to a tree above the grave with the inscription "Eliza Jane Thomas." The grave had been adorned with a variety of trinkets from many different visitors. There were things like flowers, pieces of clothing, little toys and coins. We were now at maximum spooky level.

I sat in the Jeep and pretended to play with my GPS. "Get out and look for the cache," I said to my son. I had no intention of getting out of the vehicle and going anywhere near the grave.

"Okay," he said. He jumped out with no argument and started looking for the cache. His tiredness must have given him courage. I was hoping for a quick find where he would bring me the container and I would sign the log and he could put it back while I just sat in the safety of my vehicle. No such luck. He could not find it. I had to get out.

I got out and started searching. Almost immediately, I noticed a suspicious mound of sticks off to the back left of the grave. I checked and under the sticks was the cache. I ripped the lid off and signed the log with a time of 2346. We raced back to the vehicle and jumped in. I put my key fob in the ignition and nothing. The Jeep was dead. My heart briefly stopped. We were spending the night there. We were spending the night at this creepy grave and we were going to die. Eliza Jane Thomas was going to haunt us and kill us!

I looked at the message on the dash of the Jeep. "Wrong key fob" it said. I had inserted the key fob to our truck in the ignition of the Jeep. I ripped it out and inserted the correct key fob. I sped back up the road in reverse and quickly maneuvered down the dirt road to the safety of the paved road, cell phone service and civilization. Not only had we had survived the midnight visit to the lonely grave, but we also got the First to Find!

# My First 5/5 with the B.I.G.

Rebecca Lillo
*BeccaDay*

So how did two girls from Wisconsin end up on a hike with a group of Hawaiian geocachers? It all started with a note on a cache page by me (BeccaDay).

When our family began planning our vacation to Hawaii, I did what any geocacher would do: I started looking for interesting geocaches to find. I stumbled across a 5/5 that was calling out to me, Beyond Pololu (GC1005J). It sounded like rough terrain, but amazing views and adventure!

I had recently started trying to fill in my D/T grid and I was intrigued by the ultimate combo: the 5/5! I have enjoyed many group caching experiences at home in Wisconsin, so I decided to put a note on the cache page asking if there were any locals or tourists who wanted to team up to tackle this cache. Well this started a chain reaction. First, I was contacted by someone telling me that they'd put my note out on their B.I.G. (Big Island Geocachers) Facebook group page. After that happened, I got a bunch of friend requests on both geocaching.com and Facebook from different B.I.G. members, and the planning began. They were all so friendly!

The day our plane landed on the Big Island, we were greeted with leis by the geocacher, wholagal. What a warm welcome! During our trip, we also got together with piilani7 and Kateriana, who treated us to some island cuisine, snorkeling, and some excellent geocaching sites.

Finally, it was the day of hike! I brought my 12-year-old daughter CachinKatie, and my parents from Colorado, Hikinwoman & Kwesterk along to meet up with 9 B.I.G.

We met the other members of our group in a parking lot at the top of a ridge that overlooked the valley. The view was spectacular! What would normally have been a somewhat steep but fairly easy walk down to the valley was now a slippery slide with a few roots sticking out here and there for traction, thanks to recent rain. We inched along, and I believe one or two of us ended up on their backsides.

We finally edged our way down to the valley floor and were treated to a beautiful, lush landscape that made the slipping and sliding totally worth it. We crossed the stream, and then stopped and explored Pololu Valley, admiring the view of the ocean from the black sand beach. We also grabbed the geocache that was in the valley, Under the Rainbow in Pololu Valley (GC4336). We lingered a bit in this beautiful valley, making our way over to the narrow trail that began our ascent up the next ridge, which is where the trail became much more difficult.

If this trail would have been nice and dry, it would have simply been steep switchbacks, which would have gotten the heart rate up but wouldn't have been too much of a challenge. Fortunately, there was a lot of vegetation surrounding the trail to grab hold of and to carpet the trail for traction. The B.I.G. kept telling us all about the plants and animals that were unfamiliar to us from the mainland.

We finally made it to the top of the ridge and were suddenly pummeled by biting rain and wind so strong we could hardly move. Most of the geocachers took cover under the protection of a small grove of trees, but not me; there was a cache up there! I gripped my coat tightly and leaned into the wind as I searched for the cache: Zorro's Gift GC21XDB. I found it and struggled back to the trees so that the others could sign the log. As I was putting it back in place, the wind and rain suddenly quit, and we were treated to an amazing view as the sun shined down and began to dry my soaked clothing. We sat for a few minutes on the best bench in the world before beginning the most difficult part of the trail.

We crossed over the ridge and began our descent down toward Honokane Nui Valley. After just a few switchbacks, we got to the part we all knew was coming but were trying not to think about: the ropes.

A few years back, a major mudslide had washed away a good portion of the trail, so someone had placed some ropes to aid hikers down to the valley. We went down the ropes one-by-one and very slowly. Someone remarked that the rope was "slicker than snot" because of the rain. Gripping the rope was very difficult, and just when I felt I was steady, the person below me on the rope would falter, jerk the rope, and I would be wildly grasping for something to steady me. I happened to hit an especially slippery part of the rope just when the cacher below me gave it a good tug, and I found myself rolling down the steep hill. I basically did a flip and a half, but managed to keep hold of the rope. When I finally made it down to flat ground, my legs were shaking and I had to sit and calm down for a minute. A few of the geocachers decided the ropes were too difficult for them, but everyone who attempted them made it down safely, including my daughter who barely got a speck of dirt on her. We followed the trail a little farther and then came to a second set of ropes. I must admit, there were some expletives uttered by a few of us; we were not expecting this. The second set of ropes was shorter but the descent was even steeper - it felt like almost a straight drop down.

We were then nearly at the valley floor, so we started to follow the trail toward the cache. The trail was faint as that particular section didn't get much traffic. It seemed to lead to a bamboo forest, a first for me. We headed in, and things really got tricky. The bamboo towered over us and grew so close together that it soon became very dark, and we lost all sense of direction.

We exited the bamboo into a grove of Banyan trees. At this point, we were getting close to the cache and I went into finding mode. For the most part, our group had stuck together but I charged on ahead, determined to make the find. I stepped over rock walls made by ancient Hawaiian civilizations that used to live there, and part of my mind registered how impressive that was. The rest of me was focused on hunting down the cache.

The GZ was hard to pin down as the steep valley walls and tree cover made signal pretty jumpy, but I found a large banyan tree that I was sure held the cache. I hoisted CachinKatie up so she could reach up into the crevice I pointed at. I'd never been so glad to see a 3 inch plastic container in my life!

The others soon caught up as we were signing the log. We sat around resting our weary legs, drinking water and laughing. The feeling of getting our first 5/5 was euphoric, and we were all happy to have made this find. After resting and having lunch, we wandered over to the ocean and marveled at the view of the rocky, remote beach. We all agreed that getting that spot on our statistics grid was great, but the hike itself had been the very best part and completely worth the difficulty in getting there.

Our hike back was also amazing; we were so tired at the end of it! I did smack my head on a low-hanging branch on one of the rope sections and got a bit of a bump, but that was the worst injury of the group, which isn't bad considering the terrain.

Standing at the cache we were only .9 miles away from the parking lot but that was as the crow flies: our total hike covered about 6 miles. On our way back, we again lingered in the beautiful Pololu Valley and I took coordinate markings and some notes to create an EarthCache: Pololu Valley (GC3RNM5). When we finally made it back to the parking lot, we collapsed to the ground with shaky legs. Of course, then we had to take a bunch of pictures as we had survived our adventure!

This really was Geocaching at its very finest, and I'm so glad that I got to have the experience. The hike provided breathtaking views and the terrain really was an adventure. I also got to spend time with my daughter and my parents in such a fun and challenging way, which will make for some great family stories. Finally, I got to meet some excellent geocachers from Hawaii, and I'm so glad that I got to know them. And finally, I got a 5/5 geocache!

# *Not Recommended at Night*

Brian Klinger
*KBLAST*

It was 10 pm on a Wednesday in October and I
was at home, clicking the "near your home location" link on the
geocaching website. I was clicking it for about the 10th time,
hoping this time the results would be different. They weren't.

"Honey… it's late… is this streak really that important?"

My wife responded better than I thought she would. "We've
been working on this 100 days in a row streak since August. It
wouldn't make any sense to give up now. Why don't you find
something that isn't terribly far away, and I'll go with you to
get the cache? We can make it a date night!"

I didn't think the streak mattered as much to her as it did to
me, so that was all the encouragement I needed. It was icing on
the cake that she wanted to go with me and make it a date night.
I looked for the nearest cache that would be reasonably
accessible in the evening.

I noticed the puzzle I'd been looking past for the past few
weeks and realized it was a pretty simple puzzle; one of those
where you Google the information and fill in the numbers to get
the coordinates. After about fifteen minutes I had solved the

puzzle and we were ready to go. The attributes said the cache was not recommended at night, but nowhere did it say that we couldn't do it at night. I figured if there were two of us we'd be fine, and the location didn't look too foreboding.

So we jumped in the car and headed to the location of the cache. It was in a fairly urban part of the city of Bexley, not too far from Columbus, Ohio. It was getting close to 11 pm now, so most of the normally busy establishments had closed for the evening. We parked in the relatively well-lit Kroger Supermarket parking lot and looked at the GPS. We would have to walk around a car wash toward the nearby Alum Creek, where we assumed there was a bike path of some sort. That particular area was completely unlit and there were no people around, so I was a bit nervous.

However, I was with my wife and the cache was only a few hundred feet away, so I pulled up my big boy pants and started walking confidently toward the cache, explaining how easy this cache should be once we get there.

As we were getting closer to the lit but completely abandoned car wash, a man yelled at us from seemingly out of nowhere. I was so engrossed in my GPS and feigning fearlessness in front of the woman I love that his greeting startled me enough to nearly wet myself.

"Excuse me, sir… Excuse me!"

Absolutely not. I have no interest in talking to a strange man who nearly caused me to jump into my wife's arms in fear. I looked around hoping he was talking to someone else. That's when I realized there was absolutely no one else in sight.

"Yes?" I was trying hard not to let my voice shake.

"We're not from around here. We were on our way north from Texas and we ran out of gas. We're completely on empty." He pointed over to two U-Haul trucks sitting back to back in the back corner of the Kroger parking lot. I hesitated, and he said, "If you walk over to the U-Hauls with me, I'll show you that the needle's on E."

He motioned for me to follow him, but I just stood there, still looking for any signs of life other than the man, my scared wife, and me. The guy spoke up and said, "We just need a couple of bucks, and we can be on our way."

Aha! This was my out. "I don't carry any cash with me."
I can't lie to save my life, but this was a true statement.

"But we'll be happy to drive over to a gas station, buy some gas, and bring it back to you. Did you see any open gas stations on your way over here?"

Now the guy was looking at us funny. He spoke a little more slowly and said, "If you could just give us a couple of bucks, we can be on our way." He held out his hand.

Now I spoke a little more slowly and clearly as well. "Right. I don't have any cash at all on me... so we'll be happy to go to a gas station and buy you some gas and bring it back here so we can help you out."

The guy looked at us funny again and said, "Um... I think there's one over there..." and pointed west. He also reminded us that he was in the U-Haul and he'd be waiting for us.

For about half of a second I thought about how we were going to still get the cache but my wife whirling around and heading back to the car brought me back to my senses. We got back to the car and got out of there as quickly as we could, making sure to drive west.

I drove for a little while as we talked about how odd and scary that exchange had been. After a short drive I turned around, wondering why I could never find a police officer when I needed one. We drove past the Kroger and U-Hauls were still sitting there. I even tried speeding, hoping that a police officer would suddenly appear out of nowhere so I could tell him what happened.

After driving a little while longer we actually found a police station. It was in an odd place and looked like the front lobby to a sleazy hotel, but it was our best hope.

I walked in with my wife, completely unsure if this was a police station. I was thrilled to find six or seven police officers sitting in the room, laughing and lounging around.

They looked up at us. I'm sure they were wondering what this couple was doing wandering into their police station at 11 at night. I started telling them our story and they kind of grinned and nodded, recognizing the story of a typical scam being pulled on a couple of greenhorns.

Then I got to the part where he pointed at the two U-Hauls. Suddenly they all jumped up from their seats and asked me exactly where he was. Most of them ran out the door, leaving us wondering what had just happened.

One of them remained behind and asked me for my name and number and let us know someone would call us, then he ran out the door, as well.

We went out to our car and headed east... away from that cache. We had to drive a number of miles to find the next closest cache, but we made sure it was in a well-populated and well-lit area. It was so close to midnight we hung around a little longer and got a cache for the next day, as well.

We got a call from the dispatcher later that evening. The police had arrived at the Kroger and the U-Hauls were gone. The dispatcher explained that there had been a number of recent robberies in the area where a man would lure the victims to the U-Hauls saying he was out of gas, then knock out the victims and steal everything they had, putting it all in the U-Hauls.

This was our first time ever finding ourselves in legitimate danger while geocaching, and our first time deciding to leave without even attempting the cache. It was also my first lesson in taking the attributes seriously. "Not recommended at night" was a bit of an understatement at this particular cache.

Two days later, during the day and with lots of people around, I made my way to ground zero. The bike trail was lovely, the sun was shining brightly, and there were tons of muggles all around making it difficult to retrieve the easy to find cache – and I couldn't have been happier.

# *Extras*

185

*Our Sponsor*

# Common Geocaching Terms

**Archive** – Archiving a cache removes the listing from public view on Geocaching.com. This action is usually taken when a cache owner does not intend to replace a cache after it has been removed. As an alternative to archiving, the cache owner can temporarily disable their cache if they plan to provide maintenance on the cache or replace the container within one month.

**Attribute** – These are icons on a cache detail intended to provide helpful information to geocachers who wish to find specific types of caches. These icons represent unique cache characteristics, including size, whether the cache is kid friendly, if it is available 24 hours a day, if you need special equipment and more. Attributes are also a tool to help you filter the types of caches you would like to search for when building a Pocket Query (see Pocket Query).

**Benchmark** – Using your GPS unit and/or written directions provided by NOAA's National Geodetic Survey (NGS), you can seek out NGS survey markers and other items that have been marked in the USA.

**Bookmark List** – A Premium Member feature that can be used to group cache listings in whatever way you like. You may want a bookmark list of caches you intend to find this weekend, or perhaps an "all-time favorite" list you can share with friends.

**Cache** – A shortened version of the word geocache. (See Geocache).

**Cacher** – One who participates in geocaching. Also known as geocacher.

**Caches Along a Road** – A road that has caches at every available pull-off, or nearly every pull-off. These are popular for people who like Park and Grab caches.

**Caches along a Route** – A Premium Member feature that allows you to identify caches along a specific route for quick and easy geocaching. You can choose from routes already created by other geocachers or use Google Earth to build your own unique trip.

**Caches along a Trail** – This means that there are multiple caches placed along a hiking trail. Similar to Caches along a Road, Caches along a Trail is an "easy" way to find a lot of caches in a short amount of time.

**D/T Grid (Difficulty/Terrain)** – Geocaches are rated in two categories, each designated on a 5-point scale (in half-point increments). Difficulty relates to the mental challenge of finding a geocache, while Terrain describes the physical environment. A D/T Grid is finding geocaches with all difficulties in all terrains. There are 81 possible combinations.

**Datum** – A datum is something used as a basis for calculating and measuring. In the case of GPS, datums are different calculations for determining longitude and latitude for a given location. Currently, geocaching uses the WGS84 datum.

**Dipping** – The act of logging a Travel Bug or Geocoin into a cache, and immediately logging it back into ones possession. Someone cachers "dip" a Travel Bug or Geocoin in order to register miles traveled before placing the trackable for someone else to find. Some people use a "personal traveler" to track their miles between caches, and will "dip" the traveler into each cache they find.

**Drunken Bee Dance** – The movements of a geocacher, trying to pinpoint Ground Zero, chasing the directional arrow first one direction and then another, has been termed the Drunken Bee Dance.

**EarthCache** – This is one of several unique cache types. An EarthCache is a cache that promotes geoscience education. Visitors to EarthCaches can see how our planet has been shaped by geological processes, how we manage the resources and how scientists gather evidence to learn about the Earth.

**Event Cache** – This is one of several unique cache types. Events are gatherings set up by local geocachers and geocaching organizations to meet players and to discuss geocaching.

**GC Code** – A unique identifier associated with every geocache listing. The GC Code starts with the letters "GC" and is followed by other alphanumeric characters.

**GeoArt** – A series of caches placed to form a shape. Example include hearts, a person, animal, etc. Caches may or may not be multi-stages caches.

**Geocache** – A hidden container that includes a logbook for geocachers to sign. A geocache may also include trade items.

**Geocoin** – Geocoins work similarly to Groundspeak Travel Bugs® (see Travel Bugs) in that they are trackable and can travel the world, picking up stories from geocache to geocache. Geocoins are often created as signature items by geocachers and can also be used as collectibles.

**Geomuggle** – see Muggle.

**Groundspeak** – The parent corporation for geocaching.com. Groundspeak also manages waymarking.com and wherigo.com

**Groundspeak Lackey** – A "Groundspeak Lackey" is a term used to refer to the employees and founders of Groundspeak who do the most basic tasks to support the overall needs of the community. This willingness to serve each other and provide recreation for a worldwide community is a core value of our company.

**Ground Zero** – The location at which the GPS unit is saying the geocache container is located. Also known as GZ.

**Hitchhiker** – A hitchhiker is an item that is placed in a cache, and has instructions to travel to other caches. Sometimes they have logbooks attached so you can log their travels. All trackable items can also be called a hitchhiker.

**Latitude** – Latitude and longitude create a waypoint. Latitude is the angular distance north or south from the earth's equator measured through 90 degrees.

**Letterbox** – A letterbox or letterboxing is similar to geocaching, but you use a series of clues to find a container. Once you find the container (or letterbox), you use the carved stamp from the box, stamp your personal logbook and return that stamp to the letterbox. You then use your carved stamp and stamp the letterbox's logbook.

**Longitude** – Latitude and longitude create a waypoint. Longitude is the angular distance measured on a great circle of reference from the intersection of the adopted zero meridian with this reference circle to the similar intersection of the meridian passing through the object.

**Mega-Event Cache** – This is one of several cache types. A Mega-Event cache is similar to an Event Cache but it is much larger. Among other considerations, a Mega-event cache must be attended by 500+ people. Typically, Mega Events are annual events and attract geocachers from all over the world.

**Muggle** – A non-geocacher. Based on "Muggle" from the Harry Potter series, which is a non-magical person.

**Muggled** – The discovery of a cache by a non-geocacher. Also can be termed "geomuggled". When someone refers to a cache as having been muggled, it almost always means the cache was stolen or vandalized.

**Multi-Cache** – This is one of several cache types. A multi-cache, or multiple cache, involves two or more locations, the final location being a physical container. There are many variations, but most multi-caches have a hint to find the second cache, and the second cache has hints to the third, and so on.

**Mystery or Puzzle Caches** – This is one of several cache types. The "catch-all" of cache types, this form of cache can involve complicated puzzles you will first need to solve to determine the coordinates. Examples include complicated ciphers, simple substitutions, arithmetical quizzes and clues cleverly hidden within the graphics.

**NAD27** – Stands for North American Datum 1927. The precursor to WGS84. Many maps still use the NAD27 datum , so always check before using a GPS unit with a map.

**Nano** – An unofficial cache size. A nano cache is usually considerably smaller than the typical micro. One popular container is approximately the size of an eraser on the end of a pencil.

**Officer McFriendly** – Term for an encounter with any law enforcement officer while out geocaching.

**Personal Traveler** – A trackable item that is activated but is not released. The owner of the item dips it in caches but it never leaves the owner's possession.

**Pocket Query** – (PQ) A Premium Member feature, a Pocket Query is custom geocache search that you can have emailed to you on a daily or weekly basis. Pocket Queries give you the ability to filter your searches so you only receive information on the caches you want to search for.

**Reviewer** – World-wide network of volunteers who publish the geocache after the listing is submitted to geocaching.com.

**ROT13** – Hints for geocaches are encrypted using a simple format where each of the letters are rotated 13 characters up or down in the alphabet.

**Signal** – Signal is the official mascot of geocaching.com. Designed by artist Koko, Signal is a frog with an GPS antenna on its head.

**Signature Item** – An item unique to a specific geocacher that is left behind in caches to signify that they visited that cache. These often include personal geocoins, tokens, pins, craft items or calling cards. These are acceptable trade items and may be removed from a cache.

**Souvenirs** – A souvenir is a virtual pieces of art that are most often awarded for finding a geocache in a specific geographical location or for finding a geocache on a specific day of the year. The souvenir can be displayed on your profile page, as well as on the Geocaching iPhone, Android and Windows Phone 7 apps. Geocaching artists have produced more than 100 souvenirs.

**Spoiler** – A spoiler is information gives details that can lead the next cacher to the cache. It is like an accidental hint. An example would be a post for a geocache like: "We parked right next to the log where the cache was hidden."

**Streak** – A geocaching streak is number of days in a row where the cacher has looked for and successfully discovered a geocache.

**Swag** – Are the items that are left in a geocache for trade. This is sometimes expressed as the acronym 'Stuff We All Get" however the word "swag" is not really an acronym.

**Trackable Item** – Any item that can be tracked on geocaching.com.

**Trade Item** – Items in a geocache that are available to be taken. It is a best practice that you leave an item of equal or greater value for each item you take.

**Traditional Cache** – The original cache type consisting of at least a container and a logbook. The coordinates listed on the traditional cache page are the exact location for the cache.

**Travel Bug Hotel** – A geocache with the intended purpose of acting as an exchange point for Travel Bugs. These are almost always regular or larger sized containers.

**Travel Bug®** – A Groundspeak Travel Bug is a trackable tag that you attach to an item. This allows you to track your item on Geocaching.com. The item becomes a hitchhiker that is carried from cache to cache (or person to person) in the real world and you can follow its progress online.

**Waypoint** - A waypoint is a reference point for a physical location on Earth. Waypoints are defined by a set of coordinates that typically include longitude, latitude and sometimes altitude. Every geocache listed on our website is a waypoint. Geocaching.com generates a unique "GC Code" associated with every geocache listing.

# Getting Started Geocaching

If you're reading this book as a muggle, I hope you'll consider joining us in this wonderful family-friendly game! You'll need a few items to get started:

- **GPS** – you can get a good starter unit for around $100! You really don't need anything fancy.
- **GPS App for your phone** – this has limited accuracy in the "wild" areas of the world where you're away from cell towers. The app is free and it's a great way to get started.
- **Geocaching account** – visit Geocaching.com to join. Accounts are free or you can upgrade to a premium membership and access additional features.

And really, that's it! From there, you can search for geocaches near you. Some handy things to bring with you on your adventure are:

- A pen
- Small trinkets for swag
- A "poking stick" (as Andrea Tantillo calls it)

As you're getting started on your adventures, remember that

you have to develop your "geosense" which allows you to guess where a cache might be. If you can go out with a cacher who has a few finds, that's a great way to get started and have some successes.

Please keep your common sense! Take water and snacks, tell somebody where you're going, and don't stick your fingers into strange holes – there might be a critter in there! Like any outdoor adventure, geocaching has its risks so please stay safe.

All of geocaching really relies on the honor system: you'll re-hide the cache as good or better than you found it, you will clean up after yourself (and take out "extra" trash), you'll only claim finds you actually locate, and your trade items are quality.

For more information, and to create your geocaching membership account, go to www.Geocaching.com

# A Favor to Ask...

Thank you so much for reading *Geocaching GPS: Great Personal Stories of Geocaching Firsts*! The authors and myself really appreciate your support!

As you probably know, many people look at the reviews on Amazon before they decide to purchase a book. If you liked this book, could you please take a minute to leave a review with your feedback?

60 seconds is all I'm asking for, and it would mean the world to all the authors in the book!

Thank you so much,

*Kim*

# Free Gift From Kim

Guess what! I'd like to offer you a complimentary subscription to my bi-monthly email newsletter about geocaching! This is perfect if you're just getting started in the game, but there's lots of goodies if you're a more experienced cacher too!

Go to www.FindYourGeocache.com/Subscribe to claim your free subscription!

# *About the Editor*

Kimberly Eldredge is a third generation Arizona native. She graduated from the University of Arizona with a degree in Creative Writing. She has been writing all her life and has been published in poetry journals, short story anthologies, and regional travel magazines.

In addition to loving geocaching, Kim also backpacks, kayaks, hikes, and fishes. She also enjoys cooking – especially in camp and along the trail. Kim writes a geocaching blog at www.FindYourGeocache.com

She is also fluent in Spanish and has written several children's stories in Spanish.

Kim lives in Chino Valley, Arizona.

# Other Books From Kimberly Eldredge

Geocaching GPS: Stories of Romance, Adventure, & Connection (Volume 1)
    ISBN: 978-1512258097

Scary & Silly Campfire Stories: Fifteen Tales For Shivers & Giggles (Volume 1)
    ISBN: 978-0615690902

Scary & Silly Campfire Stories: Fifteen Spooky & Silly Tales (Volume 2)
    ISBN: 978-0615701165

Scary & Silly Campfire Stories: Fifteen Scary & Silly Stories (Volume 3)
    ISBN: 978-0615741130

Pitch Your Tent: A Family's Guide To Tent Camping
ISBN: 978-1492857761

Camp Cooking 101:
101 Fun & Easy Recipes from The Outdoor Princess
    ISBN: 978-1492120476

My Camping Recipes: A Personal Collection
(A blank book to fill with your favorite camping recipes)
    ISBN: 978-1492191261

Manufactured by Amazon.ca
Bolton, ON